*I Love You—
Talk to Me!*

# I Love You— Talk to Me!

## How Couples Grow Close and Stay Close

# Donald R. Harvey

*A Raven's Ridge Book*

2746

Baker Books

A Division of Baker Book House Co
Grand Rapids, Michigan 49516

Published by Raven's Ridge Books
an imprint of Baker Book House Company
P.O. Box 6287, Grand Rapids, MI 49516-6287

Printed in the United States of America

**Library of Congress Cataloging-in-Publication Data**

Harvey, Donald R. (Donald Reid), 1948–
   I love you / talk to me! : how couples grow close and stay close / Donald R. Harvey.
      p.     cm.
   ISBN 0-8010-4399-9 (pbk)
   1. Marriage. 2. Communication in marriage. 3. Interpersonal conflict.
4. Conflict management. 5. Avoidance (Psychology)
HQ734.H363    1995
306.81—dc20
                                     95-34909

To Jan
whose constant love
nourishes my desire
to draw close

# Contents

**Part 4  Facing Our Natural Tendency to Avoid**

# Quick-Quiz Directory

# *Introduction*

The theme of *I Love You—Talk to Me!* stems from one basic and underlying assumption: We are created for intimacy. As we consider our spiritual selves, we are created to be in intimate relationship with our Creator. But the truth of intimacy extends beyond the spiritual alone to include human relationships. We are created for closeness, not isolation, and there is no relationship more representative of this than marriage.

*I Love You—Talk to Me!* is a book about intimacy. It is about what is involved in building an intimate relationship. But it is also about what often prevents this. In marriage, the pathway to intimacy is through talking. It is through talking that dissatisfactions—the hurts and frustrations that arise in every relationship—can be resolved. Failing to talk means failing to resolve. And failing to resolve ultimately results in pushing each other apart. It is also through talking that we become self-disclosing—sharing ourselves with our spouses. We share what we feel, what we think, and who we are. Through the experience of reciprocal sharing, we progressively know and are known. Love grows deeper and bonding takes place. Failing to talk in this manner allows distance to creep into a relationship. The void increases until there is little that is holding a marriage together.

*I Love You—Talk to Me!* is a book about the love that can exist in marriage and about building intimate relationships. It is also a book about *avoidance*—the all too common tendency that interferes with developing intimacy. In this regard, *I Love You—Talk to Me!* is for all couples. Though each relationship is made unique by what we as individuals bring into it, I can safely say that there is no marriage exempt from the tendency to be avoidant. None! If we are to have all that God has provided us in our marriages, we will have to successfully resolve the tendency to be avoidant.

Do not mistake *I Love You—Talk to Me!* for a book about conflict resolution or a how-to primer for those who want to learn how to fight fair. There are tasks scattered throughout the text that are meant to aid you in taking your own "marital pulse," but the real focus is not on developing a particular set of skills. Rather, it is my hope that you will experience a change of perspective.

*I Love You—Talk to Me!* gives us permission—permission to be imperfect and permission to deal with our imperfections. There is a natural difficulty that accompanies trying to talk about dissatisfactions. No one is completely comfortable with conflict. There is the added difficulty of trying to talk about things as personal as what you are feeling. This too can be uncomfortable. But if talking is the vehicle through which relationships are built, something has to be done to insure that talking occurs, often in spite of these natural interferences.

Doing what is best, as opposed to what is most comfortable, is not always easy to accomplish. This dilemma of knowing what is right, yet having difficulty doing it, is another primary emphasis in this book. We can have intimate relationships, but having marriages of this quality frequently requires something from us. We may have to change.

Change comes to a marriage when we understand what is needed to build a relationship *and* are willing to face the particular interferences that stand in our way. *I Love You—Talk to Me!* focuses on both of these areas. In it is a clear definition of marital health—what *ought* to be happening. And in it is a clear description of the most common interferences—the *whys* of our avoidance. By adapting what is presented here, you can build the kind of relationship you were created to have. You can have an intimate marriage.

# One

## The Avoidance Trap

# 1

# *The Wilsons*

## An Illustration of Avoidance

As we sat in my office, what I noticed most about the Wilsons was their countenance. They both appeared pleasant and amiable. There was not a hint of anxiety or discomfort. The interactions taking place between John and Paula were congenial and even bordered on frivolous as evidenced by an occasional outburst of laughter from Paula. She was the more expressive of the two. John would smile at something that struck him as humorous, but he was very much in control of his emotions. Something tremendously funny would be required for John to actually laugh out loud. This was hardly the atmosphere to which I was accustomed. After all, this was a marriage counselor's office. Where was the frustration? Where was the disappointment? Where was the anger?

I suspected that the display of congeniality was actually a facade. Beneath the pleasantries, truer emotions had to exist. And these truer emotions would be far less positive than the amiable and pleasant appearances that Paula and John were so artfully projecting. The passage of time in our session, coupled with some questions on my part and further discussion by John and Paula, proved my suspicion to be accurate. There was far more to the Wilsons' relationship than what met the eye.

John and Paula were both quite adept at deception. It's not that they were intrinsically dishonest. In fact, they were quite the opposite. John and Paula both had professional careers and were highly esteemed by colleagues in their respective fields. Though their public reputations were impeccable, emotional dishonesty had seemed to dictate their moods at home. Neither one talked about how they felt. They did not deal with frustrations, nor did they share honest thoughts and feelings. Instead, they operated with deception. What I was witnessing at the beginning of our session was exactly the manner in which they behaved at home—with a facade.

What brought John and Paula to counseling was a breakdown in the facade. Events had occurred in their marriage that made it difficult to continue the relationship in the manner in which they were accustomed. Paula kept breaking through their superficial layer of "everything is fine" to the truer core of her emotions. She was angry and resentful toward John. And on the occasions when she broke through the thin layer of pretense and touched her true feelings, she would unleash strong hostility on him. It was Paula's resentment toward John and John's discouragement with Paula's inability to get past her hostility that brought them in for counseling.

Paula:     It makes me so angry when I think of what he did to me.

John:      She's got to get past the hurt. I go along thinking that things are fine—that, finally, we're getting on with our lives. Then, out of nowhere, Paula erupts.

The cycle was clear. Neither liked it—but neither seemed able to interrupt it or to prevent the damage that was being inflicted on the marriage. In exasperation—almost as a final, desperate act for the salvation of their marriage—they sought counseling.

## The Buildup to Crisis

The event that so changed the dynamics of their relationship was an affair. Extramarital relationships generally throw a marriage into crisis. This was no less true for John and Paula. The discovery of the affair had been especially devastating for Paula. There had been no hint of discontent from John. Then, without warning, came the disclosure that there was another woman. Two years had passed since the traumatic day when the affair was made known. The disclosure had been followed by a few tense weeks. With some deliberation, John made the decision to end the affair and resume his marriage. Though the marriage remained intact, the legacy of the extramarital involvement seemed to tenaciously follow after them. Betrayal was a part of their past. It was history—past tense. Yet for Paula, the pain of the event was still very much in the present tense.

Two years of thinking things would be different, only to find them remaining the same, finally convinced John and Paula of the need to face their dilemma. Something had to happen. Things could not go on with unpredictable episodes of hostility. There needed to be resolution. John and Paula both feared that without a change of some kind their relationship might dissolve. Fearing the worst, they were finally ready to deal with their marriage.

There had been ample time since the disclosure of the betrayal for John and Paula to have resolved the questions and feelings that can lock mates into obsessing about an affair. But the passage of time had made little difference. John and Paula were obviously still stuck. They needed to deal with the "present tense" of their relationship. This is where we would begin. There needed to be some resolution regarding the affair. But I also wondered what had led John and Paula to this point of betrayal.

John and Paula had been married for ten years. Though the last two had been tumultuous, what could be said of the first eight? Were those early years equally problematic? Probably not! Marriages do not begin in a state of crisis. They begin positively with wonderful dreams and all the optimism in the world. When did the dreams fade for John and Paula, and what caused the loss of optimism?

## The Erosion of Love

As we began to piece together an abbreviated version of their marital history, a picture of marital failure began to emerge. There was nothing glaring or overt about what John and Paula reported. There was nothing so obvious as to catch the attention of friends or relatives. Still, though quiet and subtle, the characteristics forecasting potential failure were present from the very beginning.

John and Paula had been friends for several years before becoming romantically involved. They met at a college founded by their denomination and began to date just prior to graduation. Part of what attracted John and Paula to one another was the strong Christian commitment that each had displayed—a commitment demonstrated by daily decisions. They truly had a great deal in common.

Completing college and entering the world of work heightened their desire to be with one another. Then came a point of decision and transition. Paula was planning to enter graduate school, which would require a geographical relocation. What would this mean for their relationship?

Paula's decision to go to graduate school came as no surprise to John. Both she and John had spoken of doing so after graduation from college. They thought that a couple of years of employment experience might enhance what they would receive from further education. Going back to school was just one of those things that would happen someday—but that someday was always in the future. With Paula's decision to return to school, the future became the present. And the present was something that had to be faced.

John and Paula were not so naive as to think that graduate school would not be stressful. But they felt that their love for one another, coupled with how well they knew each other, would enable them to conquer any obstacle. After all, long before the romance a friendship had existed. So John and Paula decided to wed and to begin their married life together with Paula entering graduate school.

John was from a strongly traditional home. His father was definitely the head of the family. He took care of everything except the children. That had been John's mother's responsibility. John described his father as a good man but *too* traditional. He was stern. Emotions did not come easily to John's father, and so he projected very little warmth. Though John had desired a close relationship with his father, this seemed to be beyond his father's capability. Things such as emotions and closeness appeared uncomfortable for him. These were commodities he even failed to express toward his wife, whom he tended to dominate.

John witnessed this model for marriage and family but was determined to be different from the man who had raised him. As we will discover, though there were areas of distinct difference between John and his father, he carried more of this parental example with him than he realized.

John was soft-spoken, not at all like the father he had described earlier in our session. And in his softness was a sense that he was in touch with some deep and strong emotions, though he did not speak of feelings. There was real passion in this man.

> I wanted Paula to be a success in graduate school. I wanted her to achieve—to make it. It seemed so important to her. But she had a difficult time. So I began to do everything I could to help her. I took care of everything.
>
> Gradually, school became her life. It was like an obsession. Paula became totally goal directed. There was no balance in her life, no outside activities, and no room for me. It was as if I stopped existing. I began to resent our situation.
>
> Here I was, investing all of my energies in working and taking care of everything so that Paula had as little encumbrance as possible, and I was getting nothing in return. Nothing! She would bring study partners into our house for hours at a time. Occasionally, she would take a study break and "squeeze me in." She'd say, "We've got thirty minutes before I go back to studying. Let's make the most out of it." Paula meant this for good—but it really hurt my feelings.
>
> I felt neglected, unappreciated, and generally taken for granted. I began to resent Paula for treating me that way and I detested the whole idea of school.

As John spoke, it was obvious that he still had strong feelings about this time of rejection. There were tears in his eyes to underscore the reality of that resentment. But when I asked John what he had done in an attempt to deal with his obvious dissatisfaction, he grew silent. Finally he replied, "Not much."

> I guess I was too into taking care of Paula. I did tell her that I thought she needed more balance in her life—that she needed to

relax and not be so obsessed with school. So she probably knew I was unhappy. But I never told her how I was feeling.

At this point in John's discussion, Paula abruptly lifted her hands into the air and gave me a facial expression of complete exasperation. She then stated that she had been oblivious to any problems. Paula thought everything was fine at home. School was tough and, as she looked back at the situation, her obsessed behavior was probably foolish. But she didn't recognize any dissatisfaction on John's part.

At best, John had been giving out a very weak signal. He was admittedly upset and dissatisfied. But the best he could offer Paula was support and caring advice—advice that she should put more balance in her life. In healthy marriages, mates can say "I need" and "I feel." They are emotionally honest with each other, clearly dealing with how they are feeling and what they are thinking. But that was not the case with John and Paula. Emotional dishonesty was the overriding theme in their relationship.

After Paula finished graduate school, there would have been an opportunity for her and John to more easily deal with their marriage. After all, John could quit taking care of everything. But by then, he really wasn't in the mood. Besides, now it was his turn to go to school. John reasoned that Paula could capitalize on her advanced degree and work while he pursued his degree. So with the breadwinner roles reversed, the hecticness of their lives continued.

Given the distance that had crept into their marriage, it is not surprising that John finally found someone who seemed more interested in his feelings than Paula. John had not sought this relationship. He did not enter it with premeditation. In fact, it was totally contradictory to his strongly conservative value system. But it could have been predicted. Failing marriages are accidents waiting to happen, and John and Paula definitely had a marriage that was failing. They were failing to bond emotionally, to grow together. The incident that brought about their crisis—and that brought their marital failure to their level of awareness—could have been a number of things. It just so happened that for John and Paula, the particular incident was another woman.

At this point in our session, Paula began to provide more insight into the present nature of their situation. She spoke with more intensity than John. This was partly due to the extreme anger that still gripped her life. But this was also "her way." In Paula's family, women were strong. They were not necessarily dominant, but neither were they submissive. Paula's role models had been independent women, and she had been raised to speak her mind. She was not truly abrasive, but she was direct.

> John and I have been talking a lot during the last two weeks. I guess deciding to deal with our marriage has given us the permission we have needed to do that. There are some things that each of us has needed to say for quite some time. One thing I learned is that John has been carrying a load of disappointment around with him since the third day of our marriage. The third day! Can you believe that? And I never knew it!
>
> We were on our honeymoon, sitting on the beach, and suddenly John started talking about what he wanted me to do when he died. I didn't know whether to laugh or cry. Where in the world did that come from? And what did he mean by it? Did he think getting married was a mistake? Did he feel trapped? Was living with me going to kill him?
>
> I didn't know what was going on so I just reacted. Actually, I overreacted. I could tell John was stunned. He made a few comments trying to explain himself, but the discussion was quickly ended.
>
> I had no idea how significant that discussion was until this week. During one of our recent talks, John told me that that was his *first* and *last* attempt at trying to really open up to me—to share something deep and personal. Because of my reaction, he decided then and there to shut down emotionally. And he has shut me out ever since.

By this point in our session, some very blatant themes were beginning to emerge. There was a skeleton of sorts—a skeleton for the marriage—taking shape. Further discussions during the weeks that followed would help place flesh on the bones of this skeleton. There would be more incidents described, more examples to illustrate and confirm the particular roles enacted by John and Paula. It was a story filled with disappointment, emotional distance, and unnecessary marital deterioration.

## The Real Culprit

For ten years, John had been reluctant to either *deal* with any marital dissatisfactions or *share* anything of a personal nature with his wife. As his disappointment and resentment began to grow, so did the distance between him and Paula. But he kept everything to himself, maintaining the facade of a satisfying marriage. Paula, on the other hand, was oblivious to what was happening. Had she not been so consumed by her own life, she may have noticed the void in their relationship. But with her career to keep her preoccupied, and a husband who was weak when it came to offering signals of distress, she unsuspectingly rocked along thinking everything was okay.

I was moved by what I was hearing. It is always unfortunate when relationships do not reach their potential, and John and Paula's marriage was definitely missing the mark. But *unfortunate* is such an emotionless, nondescript term, hardly appropriate enough for the significance of the collapse of a relationship. This was more than unfortunate; it was truly saddening. The sadness I felt for John and Paula revolved around not only what they were experiencing, but also what they were missing. God designed marriage to be something beautiful—a close and intimate relationship—something that enriches the lives of two caring mates. This type of closeness was noticeably absent from the marriage of these two frustrated and hurting people.

As I sat quietly in my chair watching John and Paula interact and observing the pain on each of their faces, a sobering realization came to me: Crisis may have led them to counseling, but it was *avoidance* that led them to crisis. The pain that both John and Paula were experiencing, the resentment that each was carrying, and the hostility that each was expressing were all unnecessary. Their marriage did not have to come to this. But it had.

Though Paula was wrapped up in the crisis of their relationship—in the present tense pain of the affair—there was a sense that even she was grasping the truer culprit of their marital failure. Her comment to John at the close of our session seemed to capsulize this growing insight.

> I resent your "taking care" of the marriage. You made me believe there was nothing to fear—that there was no problem. You made me feel so secure. But that was false.
>
> You lied to me. You weren't happy. You deceived me for all those years—all those years when maybe we could have done something about it. I really, really resent you for that!
>
> I love you, John. I loved you then—and I love you now. But why didn't you just talk to me?

The affair had caused a crisis. Though the marriage as an institution had survived the disclosure, the marriage as a relationship had not. Therapy would need to begin here—with the affair and with reconciliation. The biblical requirements for this are clear. There would need to be acceptance of wrongdoing and a genuine statement of remorse. There would also need to be a commitment to the marriage and a demonstration of changed behavior. Forgiveness would then have to be both sought and extended. These are the factors that characterize reconciliation. And with genuine reconciliation achieved, healing would be allowed to occur between John and Paula. Until there was a true reconciling of the relationship, all other efforts would prove to be futile.

Though therapy would begin with reconciliation, the bulk of our work would really lie in building and rebuilding the relationship. John and Paula's marriage did not fail because of another woman. It failed because of *avoidance*. They did not talk! At least, they did not talk honestly and with depth. John and Paula's marriage failed because they would not deal with the dissatisfactions that arose in their relationship. And it failed because they would not share who they were with one another. Instead, they avoided both of these areas. Avoidance was more than an occasional incident or lone event. It was a constant companion, a pattern, a way of life. And it was this tendency to avoid that led them to the brink of destruction.

Even with a genuine reconciliation, unless the tendencies to avoid were faced and amended, the likelihood of a future failure would remain high. The particular incident bringing crisis to their marriage might not be another woman. But something similar would probably occur. For John and Paula, the future of their marriage rested on their ability to face and resolve the stumbling block brought about by avoidance. To this point in their relationship, this foe had proven to be more than a difficult opponent.

# 2

# *The Problem of Avoidance*

Much about John and Paula's marriage could be considered unique to them. That is the way with all of us. No matter how much we may want to simplify our understanding of complex people, relationships, and situations by placing them in tightly formed, conceptual boxes, there are always factors that make categorization less than perfect. However, we must also recognize that there are some benefits to identifying sameness. Frequently, elements can be generalized to populations.

The temptation to avoid, which was so evident in the marriage of John and Paula, is just such a factor. The nuances of their avoidance, the idiosyncratic ways in which it was played out in their marriage, are what was unique to them. But the temptation to avoid—as a distinct characteristic—is highly generalizable. It is something that every marriage will face. The "normalness" of avoidance as a temptation for us all will be addressed later. At this time, I want us to consider the real problem that avoidance presents to relationships: What's wrong with avoidance, anyway?

## The Real Problem

Basically, the real problem with avoidance is that it does not work. Husbands and wives do not avoid in an attempt to make things worse. No! They avoid with the intent of making things better. They think that avoidance will either reduce the present level of stress, protect someone from getting his or her feelings hurt, prevent the possibility of personal rejection, allow time to magically change whatever the situation is, or any number of other reasons. There are many seemingly plausible and legitimate rationales to support avoidant behavior. Regardless of how good these may sound, the simple truth remains—avoidance does not work.

John sought to make his marriage better by taking care of Paula and not dealing with her about his feelings of dissatisfaction. It does not seem that his avoidance made things better. Their marriage nearly disintegrated before his very eyes. John sought to spare Paula any unnecessary hurt feelings by keeping his disappointments to himself. But as her hostility and resentment showed, avoidance failed to accomplish this as well. John also sought to protect himself from possible hurt by closing himself off from Paula—by keeping his personal feelings to himself. This too failed. By keeping his feelings to himself, he may have reduced the potential for rejection *at that moment,* but he also lost the opportunity for closeness with Paula, a closeness that he desperately needed. It was the emotional distance in their relationship and his need for closeness that drove John to another woman.

Avoidance does not work. At least, it does not work in the long run. It may bring immediate and superficial relief in the short run. But the long-term consequences of avoidance are devastating to a marriage. The rationales may sound good. The behavior may be well intended. And the short-term benefits may even appear to be rewarding. But avoidance has never and will never be productive in a marriage. As illustrated by John and Paula, it will only lead to disaster.

## The Two Arenas of Avoidance

Avoidance causes difficulty in two distinct arenas. The first is conflict. It primarily involves the dissatisfactions that emerge between mates. The tendency to avoid conflict was well illustrated in the Wilsons' marriage. John was definitely feeling neglected. He was dissatisfied with what he thought was Paula's relegation of him to a low place of priority in the marriage. But rather than deal with her regarding his dissatisfaction, he chose to avoid.

Dissatisfactions are common in every marriage. The particular issue may not be feelings of neglect, like those reported by John, but every relationship will experience dissatisfactions of some kind. The degree to which these issues are honestly faced and resolved will determine whether mates are behaving in a constructive manner or whether they are allowing conflict avoidance to interfere with the growth of their relationship.[1]

The second arena of avoidance is intimacy. This term is not meant to have any sexual connotation but refers primarily to the level of self-disclosure and personal sharing between mates. Once again, the Wilsons serve as a clear illustration of this form of avoidance. Paula claimed that John had shut down emotionally. To the degree that Paula's observation was accurate, John was not being intimate with her.

Are mates sharing with one another, being open about how they feel, what they think, and who they are? Do they feel close to one another? The extent to which they are being open, as opposed to emotionally and intellectually closed, determines whether or not they are allowing *intimacy avoidance* to interfere with the growth of their relationship.

A closer look at each of these arenas will both aid our recognition of these tendencies and clarify just how avoidance interferes with the development of a healthy relationship. These insights can be extremely beneficial to the continued growth of any marriage.

### Conflict Avoidance

Conflict avoidance will not always lead a relationship to a point of crisis as it did with the Wilsons. But neither will it lead to a marriage characterized by closeness.

*Conflict* has a strong connotation. It suggests more than a mere disagreement or difference of opinion. Conflict has an emotional element, a negative emotional element. Being both *emotional* and *neg-*

*ative* leads to personal discomfort. When faced with the present reality of personal discomfort, it is easy to understand how avoidance can be an attractive alternative to actually dealing with conflict.

I do not use the term *conflict avoidance* while counseling or conducting seminars. It sounds too clinical. I prefer to turn the situation around and use the term *deal*, and I ask the simple question: "Do you *deal* with your spouse regarding your dissatisfactions?"

In one seminar I was conducting, a participant asked how she could know if she was failing to deal with dissatisfaction in her marriage. I asked if there were ever times when she would get upset with her husband. She smiled and said, "Yes." I then asked whether she dealt with him about how she was feeling when she became upset. She responded, "Sometimes I do, but frequently I do not." I then answered her initial question. "Anytime that you become upset with your husband, yet fail to deal with him regarding how you are really feeling, you are being avoidant. The rule of thumb in my home is this: 'If it is significant enough to get upset about, it is significant enough to deal with.'"

I focused on the issue of becoming upset purely as an illustration. Dissatisfaction is a broad term that can encompass a variety of situations. To think only in terms of becoming upset would greatly limit our understanding of conflict avoidance. For example, you may find yourself in a situation where there is disagreement or a lack of cooperation. This may result in frustration. Or, there may be something that was supposed to have happened but didn't, which may result in disappointment. There may be a careless word, a neglectful behavior, or an insensitive attitude. These may result in hurt. Each of these situations is different, and each can cause an extensive range of possible emotional responses. But each represents a dissatisfaction that must be dealt with.

When your spouse frustrates you, what do you do?
When your spouse disappoints you, what do you do?
When your spouse hurts your feelings, what do you do?

Think about these questions. How would you answer them? Your response will indicate whether you are being avoidant. Do you physically withdraw instead of dealing directly with your mate when you are frustrated by something that he does? Do you simply ignore a slight, choosing to pretend that it did not occur? Do you rationalize the pain from harsh words, telling yourself that it really doesn't matter anyway? Do you refuse to talk about your feelings but let your spouse know of your displeasure in other ways? If you do any of these, you are being avoidant. Anything short of dealing honestly, directly, and appropriately is conflict avoidant behavior.

The real problem for couples who fail to deal with dissatisfactions is not the behavior itself, but the consequences that the behavior has on the relationship. Conflict avoidance pushes spouses apart and blocks emotional closeness. This pushing apart and blocking was clearly illustrated by John and Paula. Ever increasingly as John failed to deal with his dissatisfactions, the void between him and Paula grew larger and larger. Resentment pushed him away from the woman he loved. By the time their situation changed enough to allow them the opportunity to more easily deal with their relationship, John was no longer in the mood. He was blocked. It is easy to see how these by-products of failing to deal with dissatisfactions significantly work against the ultimate goal of marriage—to draw close.

Being pushed apart and blocked is the work of resentment—and resentment is the primary consequence of failing to deal with dissatisfactions. I refer to resentment as historical anger or "anger with a history." There is nothing inherently wrong with anger. Paul's admonition to those in the church at Ephesus illustrates this: "If you are angry, do not let anger lead you into sin" (Eph. 4:26).

According to Paul's comments, we can be both angry and sinless. What differentiates the two seems to be what we do with our anger. Though it could be argued that avoidance, in and of itself, is not necessarily sinful behavior, avoidance definitely brings us into contradiction with Paul's further admonition: "Do not let sunset find you still nursing it [anger]; leave no loop-hole for the devil" (Eph. 4:26–27).

Paul's words echo those of Jesus who strongly criticized anyone who nurses anger against a brother (see Matt. 5:22). Nursing, harboring, failing to deal with—these are the elements that allow anger to fester and to be transformed from a natural emotion to something both devious and detrimental. And all are examples of avoidance.

Paul saw anger as an emotion that was just as natural and God-ordained as joy or happiness. But it could become a problem if it was not dealt with correctly, if it was allowed to become historical. What then is the solution? Presumptuously, I would paraphrase Paul's advice in this manner: "Do not give your anger a chance to fester. Do not nurse it. Do not allow it to turn into resentment. Deal with it. And do so quickly."

Had John followed Paul's advice, he would have dealt with Paula regarding his dissatisfactions, he would have resolved the anger that was prompted by his frustrations and hurt feelings, and he would not have developed the resentment toward Paula that pushed them apart. Instead, John chose to avoid the conflict. He chose not to deal with Paula at all, and the result was a marital crisis.

## Intimacy Avoidance

I saw Gerald at the request of a colleague. Gerald had left his wife several months earlier with the intent of getting a divorce. He was not willing to see a counselor at that time, but his wife, Kay, had the desire to do everything she could to save her marriage. Consequently, she sought the advice of a Christian professional. Gerald had initiated divorce proceedings when he left Kay, but he then placed the entire process on hold. With the passage of time and Gerald's hesitancy to proceed with the divorce came his willingness to at least talk with a counselor. However, he did not want to see the same person with whom Kay had already developed a professional relationship, so I was contacted as an alternative.

Gerald was cordial at our first meeting, but it did not take long for his feelings about his wife and his marriage to be revealed. He made statements such as "She really hurt me" and "I don't think I could ever get over it" and displayed emotions to back up his words. Whenever we got on the subject of Kay, Gerald's jaw would tighten and his eyes would become intensely focused. Gerald had some strong bitterness. It was important to determine exactly why he felt so adamant.

As Gerald related his view of their marital history, he included several acts of insensitivity on Kay's part. These were mostly in the form of rejections, slights, and discountings. As the years passed in their marriage, Gerald found himself beginning to resent Kay for the way she treated him. But what was noticeably absent from Gerald's story was the mentioning of any effort on his part to deal with his dissatisfactions. When I asked Gerald how he had chosen to deal with Kay regarding these issues, my suspicions were confirmed. Throughout eight years of marriage, Gerald's primary mode of dealing with relational frustrations and hurt was to simply withdraw—both physically and emotionally. He carefully avoided any direct confrontation.

Spouses who resentfully leave a marriage, as Gerald had done, usually do so with a sense of justification. They feel as though there is ample and legitimate reason for their departure. Their reason is tied to their perception of how they have been (mis)treated. Commonly, they are so focused on what has been done to them that they fail to recognize their own inappropriate behavior. Part of getting a mate to the place where he is willing to constructively deal with his marriage is helping him to recognize his own contributions to the marital deterioration. That was my goal with Gerald. I needed to chip away at his pious justification.

Chipping away attitudes of justification can be a slow and arduous process. I began by asking Gerald what he would identify as *his* contribution to this marital failure. This was not a question for which Gerald was prepared. He was far more comfortable pointing out Kay's shortcomings than trying to recognize any of his own. After a few moments, I began to give Gerald a little help by suggesting that his failure to deal directly with Kay may have contributed significantly to the deteriorated condition of his marriage. Gerald gave mental assent to what I was suggesting, but it was apparent that he was not yet ready to accept any personal responsibility for the status of his marriage. After a few more sessions, however, Gerald was at least willing to sit down with Kay to discuss the possibility of reconciling.

That first joint session was quite tense—with two angry counselees and one nonpartisan therapist. Gerald was angry with Kay for the years of insensitivity she had displayed. Kay was angry with Gerald for the cold and callous manner in which he had just walked away from her and their children. "He wasn't even going to give me a chance to work on the relationship," she lamented. But after a few weeks of fairly intense meetings, feelings began to soften. Gerald and Kay were finally able to genuinely reconcile their marriage.

Although reconciliation marked a turning point in their treatment, it did not bring an end to therapy. It merely allowed us to begin the work of restoration. We had already identified each one's wrongdoing—Kay's insensitivity and Gerald's avoidance. We then identified what should be happening in a growing Christian marriage. Recognizing what was right and what was wrong, coupled with sincere ownership of their own contributions, made working on the marriage an exciting experience.

One of the blessings of being a marital therapist is the opportunity to witness restoration. Kay and Gerald's relationship was making some tremendous headway. Not only were they reporting improvement, but it was obvious from the way they related in my office that genuine changes had occurred in their marriage. Then, at the beginning of one of our sessions, Kay spontaneously made an interesting announcement.

> Things are going very well. We're dealing with dissatisfactions as they arise and actually resolving them. Our relationship is better than it's ever been. But I don't feel intimate with Gerald. We're just not close.
>
> We don't really share anything meaningful. I wanted to talk about something spiritual the other night but was afraid to approach Gerald. Here, we're both Christians, yet we can't talk about anything spiritual. And it extends far beyond that.

I was not surprised with Kay's comments. In fact, this other arena was an area of their marital life that I had planned to address when I felt they were ready to do so. They just got ready a little sooner than I had expected. Even though conflict avoidance had been changed, intimacy avoidance was still a problem. The resentment that had been blocking and pushing them apart had diminished, and they had constructively adapted the old avoidance strategies to prevent its return. Gerald and Kay were successfully dealing with dissatisfactions, but they had not done anything to help pull themselves together. This latter commodity—pulling together—is what allows mates to bond, to feel close. It is intimacy.

In my work with couples, I seldom use the term "intimacy avoidance." Instead, I turn the situation around and refer to this aspect of marriage as *talking* and ask the question, "Do you really *talk* to your spouse?" Talking, in this sense, is self-disclosing, sharing how you feel, what you think, and who you are. It entails more than superficial conversation—it requires depth. It also involves some risk. After all, to be superficial is to be safe; to share something as personal and private as feelings is to set yourself up for possible rejection, misunderstanding, non-acceptance, and other hurt. None of these seem attractive. But failing to self-disclose—being intimacy avoidant—also has its consequences. The primary consequence is emotional distance in the marriage. You cannot feel close unless you share.

The failure to talk was present in the marriage of John and Paula. Remember how John had shut down emotionally? But it was more clearly illustrated by Kay and Gerald. Kay's spontaneous observation capsulized the problem, "We don't really share" and "We just aren't close." Because Kay and Gerald were ready to deal with this area in their marriage, we were able to focus on some of the reasons for their failure to talk. It wasn't long before they were able to make as significant an improvement in the arena of talking as they had in the arena of dealing.

Avoidance as a temptation is two-dimensional. It tempts in the area of dissatisfaction and is also a problem in the area of sharing. This two-dimensional assault on marital stability was demonstrated in both of the relationships presented. Kay and Gerald's ability to successfully face the interferences in both of these arenas transformed their marriage from one that was deteriorating to one that was moving toward intimacy. Whenever a transformation of this type is accomplished, the relationship is strengthened. A marriage that successfully resolves avoidance tendencies approaches what marriage was intended to be—intimate.

# 3

# A Problem for Us All

"I love you—Talk to me" is a cry of the heart. It is a plea for the survival of a marriage. These were Paula's words as she pleaded with John. Their need was clearly evident. But I believe the theme expressed by her words is one shared by many.

John and Paula presented a marriage in crisis. As such, their situation could easily be described as an extreme. Most of us who do not have marriages in a state of crisis might find it difficult to identify with the Wilsons' situation. Yet we must not cast their story aside too easily. One thing my years as a marital therapist have taught me is this: No marriage begins as an extreme. Extremes are merely situations that have reached the end of a journey. Situations do not begin as they end. They move progressively from one point to the next.

Each marriage is on a journey—an adventure. The situation depicted by the Wilsons serves to underscore the process nature of this journey. John and Paula did not begin their marital journey in crisis—as an extreme. They entered marriage much like you did, with enthusiasm and optimism for the future. They desired many of the same things as you. But over time—through process—things began to change. Their relationship began to move in a hazardous direction. Not all at once, but event by event. Progressively, their adventure became perilous. Finally, there was a crisis.

Many of you would not place yourselves in the same category with John and Paula, whether referring to your marriage or to your individual behavior. You visualize your situation as far more normal—as ordinary. You view your relationship as stable; you have a good marriage. And you would also describe your behavior as less avoidant than John's. This may all be true. But even though John's avoidant behavior was excessive, and though the extent of relational erosion for John and Paula is far beyond your own, there are similarities between the Wilsons' and many marriages today. The real difference may be only a matter of degree, which in many instances does not hinder the ultimate outcome. It only affects the amount of time required to bring a journey to completion.

I do not believe that John and Paula were all that abnormal. In fact, their beginning was rather ordinary. Avoidance just got in their way. However, avoidance is not an issue that confronts some couples while completely bypassing others. It is a problem with which we *all* must contend. It is true that avoidance may present more difficulty for some than it will for others. And we may want to view John and Paula's marriage as exceptional. But this would be an inaccurate assessment. Their relationship is exceptional only because of the extent to which they allowed it to deteriorate. It was not the *presence* of avoidance that made their relationship exceptional—it was the dire *consequence*.

All couples will be confronted with a wide assortment of interferences to marital growth. Some of these will be obvious; others will be subtle. So temptations to be avoidant will not be the only interferences confronting a marriage, but they will definitely be a part of the onslaught. The extent to which interferences are successfully resolved—regardless of the form in which they appear—will determine whether a relationship will experience all that God has intended or will be merely another marriage of mediocrity or will end in crisis.

## Taking Your Pulse

To make the issue of avoidance a little more personal and a little less theoretical, take a few moments and respond to the following statements. Consider this a mini pulse-taking exercise for your marriage. Each statement reflects either a manner of dealing with the dissatisfactions that arise in your relationship or a way in which you handle talking (sharing).

Be honest! You are the only one who will see the results. There are five responses from which to choose (from *Strongly Disagree* to *Strongly Agree*). After carefully reading the statement and examining your own marriage, select the response that best reflects your level of agreement—how much the statement accurately describes how you relate to your spouse most of the time. Place the number in the space provided next to each statement. This exercise will not allow you to compile any type of score or measurement of your relationship, but you should receive a quick pulse or general feel for what you are doing in your marriage. An answer key is located at the end of this chapter.

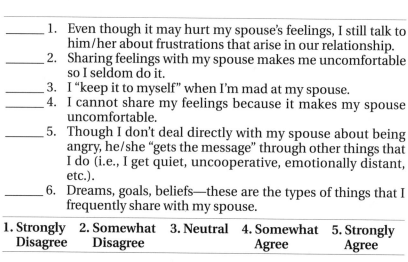

_____ 1. Even though it may hurt my spouse's feelings, I still talk to him/her about frustrations that arise in our relationship.

_____ 2. Sharing feelings with my spouse makes me uncomfortable so I seldom do it.

_____ 3. I "keep it to myself" when I'm mad at my spouse.

_____ 4. I cannot share my feelings because it makes my spouse uncomfortable.

_____ 5. Though I don't deal directly with my spouse about being angry, he/she "gets the message" through other things that I do (i.e., I get quiet, uncooperative, emotionally distant, etc.).

_____ 6. Dreams, goals, beliefs—these are the types of things that I frequently share with my spouse.

| 1. Strongly Disagree | 2. Somewhat Disagree | 3. Neutral | 4. Somewhat Agree | 5. Strongly Agree |
|---|---|---|---|---|

How did you fare? (Compare your responses with the "ideal responses" listed in the answer key at the end of this chapter.) Were all of your answers in the extreme range (*Strongly Disagree* or *Strongly Agree*) or were some of your responses more moderate? The statements are listed in a prescribed order. The odds (1, 3, and 5) represent conflict avoidant tendencies and the evens (2, 4, and 6) address intimacy avoidance. Did you find some statements more difficult to respond to than others? Is there a pattern? Are your responses to the conflict avoidant statements better or worse than those to the intimacy avoidant statements? (A "better" answer is one that approaches the ideal response listed in the answer key. It reflects a tendency to either deal or talk.) These subtle differences can provide you with valuable information regarding your marriage.

Having examined your own behavior, it is time to focus on the tendencies of your spouse. How does he/she behave in the marriage? If your mate were to respond to the same mini pulse-taking exercise that you just completed, what would be the results? You might ask him/her to do just that, and then the two of you could compare your findings. This exercise usually leads to an interesting dialogue between marital partners. But before you do, you might like to answer these questions regarding your spouse's tendencies from your point of view. How would you rate your mate?

To enable you to rate your mate, I have adapted each of the six statements. Respond to each of these as you did in the previous exercise, by selecting the response that best reflects how your spouse relates to you in your marriage. Place the number in the space provided next to each statement.

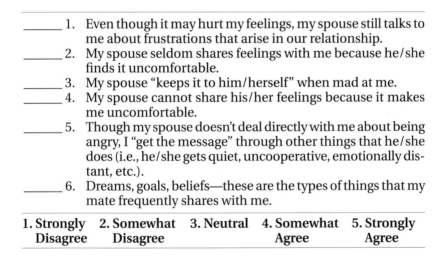

_____ 1. Even though it may hurt my feelings, my spouse still talks to me about frustrations that arise in our relationship.

_____ 2. My spouse seldom shares feelings with me because he/she finds it uncomfortable.

_____ 3. My spouse "keeps it to him/herself" when mad at me.

_____ 4. My spouse cannot share his/her feelings because it makes me uncomfortable.

_____ 5. Though my spouse doesn't deal directly with me about being angry, I "get the message" through other things that he/she does (i.e., he/she gets quiet, uncooperative, emotionally distant, etc.).

_____ 6. Dreams, goals, beliefs—these are the types of things that my mate frequently shares with me.

| 1. Strongly Disagree | 2. Somewhat Disagree | 3. Neutral | 4. Somewhat Agree | 5. Strongly Agree |
|---|---|---|---|---|

As with the previous exercise, an answer key is provided at the end of the chapter. You should be able to obtain a feel from your responses for how your mate relates or avoids. Do the two of you respond equally well (or equally poorly) or do you seem to differ? Are there differences in strengths and weaknesses? Were there any surprises?

Relationships are cooperative arrangements that to be healthy require the efforts of both spouses—not just one. That is why it is important to determine the role played by each spouse in either dealing with or avoiding conflict and intimacy. The healthy behavior of one spouse will not totally nullify the unhealthy behavior of the other.

## How Normal Is Avoidance?

The brief pulse-taking exercise that you just completed was adapted from a more extensive questionnaire created for married couples. The complete version measures not only the presence of avoidant behavior in relationships but also the motivation for such behavior. With it we are able to assess both the whats and the whys of avoidance in marriages.

I have found this questionnaire very useful in my counseling practice. For this book, I conducted a survey using the questionnaire but did not limit it to only those in counseling. I also included couples who had never needed a therapist. To reflect the diversity that characterizes the American population at large, I procured responses from a wide variety of people. There were newlyweds and not so newly weds, young and old, and couples in other than first marriages. My findings are interesting, to say the least. They are also informative and useful.

What follows is a synopsis of what I have learned regarding avoidance tendencies in marriage. I have organized these discoveries around six general themes. Each theme will be in the form of a statement and followed by a brief explanation. I am indebted to those couples who were willing to allow me—an outsider—into their marriages to witness how they relate to one another.

### 1. No one is perfect.

The most significant discovery was the confirmation of my belief that no one is perfect. Whether individually or relationally, in one way or another we all deviate from the ideal. After completing the pulse-taking exercise, this little bit of enlightenment probably comes as no surprise. I doubt that either you or your spouse had perfect scores. Now, I am the first to point out that not being perfect and not being healthy are two different issues. But the deviation from perfection in my survey did underscore that, even in healthy and ordinary relationships, avoidance is an issue that must be contended with. It's not simply a situation where *the other guy* has the problem. It is a problem for all of us.

In my survey, the tendency to be less than perfect was demonstrated by a wide variance in recorded scores. Similar to the range of choices in your pulse-taking exercise, couples in my sampling responded to the accuracy of statements regarding their marriage by indicating a level of agreement from *Strongly Disagree* to *Strongly Agree*. The statements were written in such a manner that to be ideal, a mate would sometimes respond in total agreement and at other times in total disagreement. For instance, the statement "When hurt or frustrated by something that my mate has done, I tell him/her honestly how I feel" is an example of a non-avoidant behavior. Ideally, this is the type of action that would result when a mate is confronted with dissatisfaction. So a response of *Strongly Agree* would be appropriate. Similarly, the statement "I find it uncomfortable to share my feelings with my mate" is an example of avoidant behavior. Ideally, this would not be a problem in a marriage. So a response of *Strongly Disagree* would be appropriate. Depending on the unique characteristics of a given marriage, any of the five choices might accurately describe the relationship, but only one selection for each statement would be considered ideal.

My point is this: If mates were responding to the questionnaire honestly and if their responses were to indicate ideally appropriate choices, they would have endorsed the statements in not only the correct direction (whether toward agreement or disagreement), but also in extremes (*Strongly Disagree* or *Strongly Agree*). What I actually found was quite a spread on responses. There were no perfect scores—no one suggested that avoidance was being ideally handled in his/her relationship. There were some extremes—*Strongly Disagrees* and *Strongly Agrees*. But there were far more moderate-range responses of *Somewhat Disagree, Neutral,* and *Somewhat Agree*.

There were even some statements marked in totally the wrong direction. In these instances, mates were agreeing to statements when they should have been disagreeing, and disagreeing when they should have been agreeing.

As I stated earlier, I do not believe that perfection and healthy behavior are necessarily the same thing. You can be less than perfect and still be considered healthy. But there was enough variation in the scores to suggest that, even for us normal folks, avoidance tendencies operate in our marriages. Even in those relationships where the tendency is to be emotionally honest and direct, it is difficult to always maintain consistency. We may respond in an appropriate manner one day and a totally different manner the next. In the best of marriages, the difference between full-blown avoidance and non-avoidance is simply a matter of degrees.

## 2. Avoidance does operate in two arenas.

Over the years of my involvement with couples, I have observed that avoidance tendencies operate in two distinct areas: conflict and intimacy. Because of this belief, the assessment inventory was constructed to measure behavior and motivation in each of these arenas. For example, the following statements represent the type utilized in the more extensive questionnaire. Conflict avoidant statement: "Even though it may hurt my mate's feelings, I still talk to him/her about frustrations that arise in our relationship." Intimacy avoidant statement: "I frequently share my thoughts and ideas with my mate."

Obviously, I could be wrong. Couples could tend to be avoidant only when needing to deal with dissatisfactions. Or, they could be tempted to be avoidant only when dealing with emotionally laden topics. If either one of these possibilities were true—if it were an either/or situation—I would then have expected to receive endorsement of statements in one area or the other, but not in both. So what have I found?

According to the couples who have completed the questionnaire, avoidance is a problem in both arenas, not just one. Though there are differences between couples and even between spouses, both conflict and intimacy arenas were found to present challenges and temptations for all marital relationships.

### 3. We may be better in one arena than we are in the other.

We have established that avoidance operates in two distinct arenas: one involving dissatisfactions and the other emotional closeness. Though some mates operate equally well (or equally poorly) in each of these arenas, the majority of us display a little more imbalance than that. We either do better with relational conflict *or* we do better with intimacy.

To add further confusion, the imbalances of the partners in a marriage do not always match. For example, if a husband and a wife are both uncomfortable with closeness (intimacy) issues, but are both very comfortable when it comes to dealing with relational dissatisfactions (conflict), there is consistency in their imbalance. Though intimacy will be an area warranting attention in their marriage, there will be little need to deal with tendencies to avoid conflict. However, if a husband is very direct in how he handles dissatisfaction but shies away from self-disclosure and his wife is just the opposite, avoiding conflict and pursuing closeness, the differences only serve to exacerbate their problem. In their marriage, attention to both arenas would be warranted. A seminar participant once stated it this way: "I do anger real well. It's the sharing that gives me a problem. For my wife, it's just the opposite. We never seem to get in sync."

What this husband was stating is a genuine issue for marriage. It reaffirms that marriage is a relationship. One mate's characteristics will definitely impact his spouse. Even if one partner was very proficient in dealing with both conflict and intimacy issues, there would be difficulties in the relationship unless his mate was also proficient in both of these areas. If one mate has a problem, both will have a problem. That's the way marriages work.

### 4. There are differences in how we avoid.

Another theme evidenced through responses was that mates do not always avoid conflict or intimacy in the same manner. If I were to descriptively define behavior that was non-conflict avoidant, it would be *to deal directly, honestly, and appropriately with dissatisfactions in a relationship.* A violation of any part of that definition would qualify as conflict avoidant behavior. This is important to realize. Sometimes mates fail to see themselves as conflict avoidant because they only recognize a narrow range of behavior as being avoidant. They then reason that because they do not display these specific behaviors, they must not be avoidant. These mates fail to recognize that avoidance can be displayed in many varied forms. For this reason, several statements, each identifying a different means of avoidance, were included in the questionnaire.

Let's look at two of the statements for further clarification: "I keep it to myself when I'm mad at my spouse." "Though I don't deal directly with my spouse about being angry, he/she gets the message through other things that I do (i.e., I get quiet, uncooperative, withhold affection, etc.)."

Agreeing with either of these statements indicates an avoidance of conflict. Each contradicts my description of healthy interpersonal behavior regarding matters of dissatisfaction. However, they do so quite differently. Whereas the first statement has flavors of pretending, denial, and emotional dishonesty, the latter is far more aggressive, but in a very indirect and resistant manner.

A mate could disagree with the first of these statements and, therefore, not recognize himself as conflict avoidant. However, he may find that he frequently demonstrates the second statement. This was exactly how many of the respondents answered. I listed statements that allowed for conflict and intimacy to be avoided in several different ways. Usually, mates reported tendencies to utilize specific strategies while totally rejecting others. But the end result was the same.

Avoidance is avoidance, regardless of the means used. Whether you choose to smile and deny that anything is really the matter, rationalize the problem away by telling yourself that it really isn't important anyway, or withdraw in a huff and refuse to talk about whatever it is that has upset you, the result is the same. You have avoided dealing with the situation and, as a consequence, allowed a foothold for resentment that can be disastrous for a marriage.

## 5. There are differences in why we avoid.

When we are describing behavior, we are talking about the whats. When a person does something, whatever he or she does is clearly identifiable. For example, a husband may physically withdraw from a conversation when his wife begins talking about how she feels. We can witness the withdrawal—we actually see it happen. When our focus turns from behavior to motivation, we move from the *whats* to the *whys*.

There can be many different reasons or motivations for any observed behavior. For example, the husband mentioned above who physically withdrew from a conversation with his wife could have been motivated to do so because of a personal discomfort with emotional issues in general. He may find it difficult to talk to anyone about feelings—much less his wife. Or, it could have been related to his view of roles. He may believe that men are supposed to be like John Wayne—they are to never share emotions. These are just two of several possible reasons for intimacy avoidant behavior.

A mate's behavior may be clearly identified as avoidant, which is the easier of our tasks. But what is the reason for his behavior? That can be difficult to determine. I remember speaking with a client whose wife was totally frustrated with his refusal to deal with any dissatisfactions. Not only would he not approach her regarding any dissatisfaction he might have, but he also refused to discuss any concerns that she would bring to him. As you might well imagine, this wife was absolutely exasperated with her husband's behavior. I asked him why he was so conflict avoidant. This was his response.

I'm afraid of her reaction. I cannot stand for anyone to be disappointed in me—especially Marie. I've always had a problem with disapproval.

It's hard to deal with dissatisfactions—whether they're mine or whether they're Marie's—without running the risk of her becoming upset with me. It's just not a risk I want to chance.

Though there were actually several motivations operating in support of his avoidant behavior, the one that he described to me on that occasion is called self-protection. He was fearful of how his wife might respond toward him should they get into a disagreement. In order to avert any potential for rejection or rebuff, he avoided dealing with dissatisfactions of any kind altogether.

This motivation for avoidance is not uncommon. But changing this motivation would require a different tack than if his reason for avoiding conflict was related to a fear of hurting his wife's feelings. The excessive fear of hurting another person's feelings is called over-protection and is a far different reason for avoidance than the self-protective rationale that was just illustrated by my client.

As we will discover in later chapters, there are several possible motivations for either avoiding conflict or avoiding intimacy. We do not all do the same things in our marriages. Even when there are similarities in some of our actions, they may be for entirely different reasons. It is imperative that we identify *why* we do *what* we do if the behavior is going to be changed. Corrective efforts can be futile unless motivations are clearly recognized.

### 6. Mates do not always agree on their avoidant behavior.

One advantage of having both mates complete a questionnaire is that it allows them an opportunity to discuss those areas in which deficiencies are reported, reasons for these deficiencies, and possible action plans for correcting and changing what is happening. One of the more interesting findings, however, is the difference in how the couple actually views each other's behavior.

Each questionnaire allows a spouse to describe not only his own behavior, but also the behavior of his partner. Since questionnaires are completed by both partners, a cumulative graph of results allows for a comparison between how a mate views himself with how he is viewed by his spouse. It is not unusual for there to be disagreement in these two perspectives. Usually, the difference of opinion occurs when mates view themselves in a better light than do their partners.

A common example of this disagreement is a couple's rating the husband's ability to relate on an intimate level, where he reports his behavior as only mildly avoidant, but she describes him as an exceptionally emotionally closed individual. Obviously, these marital partners would not be viewing the husband's behavior in the same light.

Disagreements in assessment such as the one just illustrated usually do not prove to be problematic but are actually helpful. These discoveries present the opportunity for honest discussion and frequently lead to constructive changes in relationships.

## Summary

Whether based on my experience as a marital therapist and observations of how couples interact in their relationships or the more concrete responses provided on an instrument created to measure avoidance, it is clear that avoidance is a problem for us all. Whether in the arena of conflict, where we are faced with relational dissatisfactions, or in the arena of intimacy, where the issues of closeness reside, no couple is exempt from facing the temptation to be avoidant. We may avoid in different manners and for different reasons, but none of us is perfect.

The real question is not whether we will face these arenas. Each of us will encounter and grapple with the temptation to avoid. Neither is the real question whether what we do in these arenas will influence our marriages. There are consequences associated with everything we do. The consequences of being conflict avoidant are different from those of intimacy avoidance. Whereas one blocks and actually pushes mates apart, the other prevents them from bonding—from pulling together. The real question is, "What will our choice be?" Will we choose avoidance or will we choose health?

For most of us, our marital journey is not yet complete. There are more roads to be taken, more dissatisfactions to possibly not deal with, and more feelings to potentially not share. Without a decision for health, we too may arrive at the same destination as John and Paula and be counted among the extremes. And even if stealthy maneuvering allows us to miss the extremes, how narrow will the margin be? I do not think it is our goal to narrowly miss disaster. Rather, it is to experience the best that God has for us.

# Key to Taking Your Pulse Exercise

All responses listed below the statements are ideal.

_____ 1. Even though it may hurt my spouse's feelings, I still talk to him/her about frustrations that arise in our relationship.

_____ 2. Sharing feelings with my spouse makes me uncomfortable so I seldom do it.

_____ 3. I "keep it to myself" when I'm mad at my spouse.

_____ 4. I cannot share my feelings because it makes my spouse uncomfortable.

_____ 5. Though I don't deal directly with my spouse about being angry, he/she "gets the message" through other things that I do (i.e., I get quiet, uncooperative, emotionally distant, etc.).

_____ 6. Dreams, goals, beliefs . . . these are the types of things that I frequently share with my spouse.

| 1. Strongly Disagree | 2. Somewhat Disagree | 3. Neutral | 4. Somewhat Agree | 5. Strongly Agree |
|---|---|---|---|---|

### Rating your own behavior:

1. Strongly Agree (5)    [conflict statement]
2. Strongly Disagree (1)    [intimacy statement]
3. Strongly Disagree (1)    [conflict statement]
4. Strongly Disagree (1)    [intimacy statement]
5. Strongly Disagree (1)    [conflict statement]
6. Strongly Agree (5)    [intimacy statement]

_____ 1. Even though it may hurt my feelings, my spouse still talks to me about frustrations that arise in our relationship.
_____ 2. My spouse seldom shares feelings with me because he/she finds it uncomfortable.
_____ 3. My spouse "keeps it to him/herself" when mad at me.
_____ 4. My spouse cannot share his/her feelings because it makes me uncomfortable.
_____ 5. Though my spouse doesn't deal directly with me about being angry, I "get the message" through other things that he/she does (i.e., he/she gets quiet, uncooperative, emotionally distant, etc.).
_____ 6. Dreams, goals, beliefs . . . these are the types of things that my mate frequently shares with me.

| 1. Strongly Disagree | 2. Somewhat Disagree | 3. Neutral | 4. Somewhat Agree | 5. Strongly Agree |
| --- | --- | --- | --- | --- |

**Rating your spouse's behavior:**

      1. Strongly Agree (5)     [conflict statement]
      2. Strongly Disagree (1)     [intimacy statement]
      3. Strongly Disagree (1)     [conflict statement]
      4. Strongly Disagree (1)     [intimacy statement]
      5. Strongly Disagree (1)     [conflict statement]
      6. Strongly Agree (5)     [intimacy statement]

# 4

# *I Believe . . .*

Janie was unhappy. Though she managed to force an occasional smile and made a concerted effort to maintain her composure, it was of little use. The tears that so freely flowed as she described her reason for contacting me for an appointment communicated more meaning than the manufactured smiles. Janie was frustrated with her marriage. But frustration with Mark was nothing new; it seemed to have been a long-time companion during their twenty years of marriage. What was new was Janie's degree of frustration and, with her increased level of intensity, Mark's response.

Things have really deteriorated during the past six months. For as long as I can remember, I've been the family cheerleader. I've tried to be a lifeline to Mark, for both the children and me. He is so wrapped up in his work that he barely has time for the family. When he does squeeze us in, it's always around something that *he* likes to do. We go along just to be with him.

The same has been true for the marriage. Mark seems so distant from me. I've had to press and press for us to do anything together. But this aloofness exceeds far beyond activities alone. It even includes simple conversation. Mark is a quiet man. If I didn't initiate conversation, I don't know if anything would be said. When he does talk, it's in partial sentences. I'm supposed to piece together what he wants, thinks, intends, . . . whatever.

I found myself constantly in the role of trying to get something happening—communication, activity, anything to suggest there was a pulse somewhere in the family and the marriage! At least I tried until six months ago. That was when I finally decided to give up the role. I just got too tired of making a statement only to hear silence—of talking to an empty room. I quit. Since then, things have really gotten tense.

Mark keeps asking what's wrong with me: "Why are you behaving this way?" He's referring to the way I've pulled back from family activities and no longer initiate conversation. He thinks I hate him. I may be angry with him—but I don't hate him. I just couldn't handle the role any longer.

My pulling back has gotten more of a response from Mark than twenty years of talking (asking, encouraging, pleading, and on occasion hollering). But all of Mark's efforts are negative. He's not trying to make any changes for himself. He really doesn't want things any different than they've always been. He just wants things back the way they were. Mark's trying to force me back into the role of the family cheerleader. I'm just not willing to go back to the way it was.

Janie described a scenario that I had heard many times before. The names and events may have been different, but the personalities were much the same. Janie had married for companionship only to find that her husband preferred to invest his energies in activities outside of the home. Whereas she desired emotional closeness and talking, Mark preferred distance and silence. Her response? "I can make it happen. If I'm just nice enough, pleasing enough, perky enough, giving enough . . . I can bring life to this marriage. Mark will give me what I need." Twenty years of being nice, pleasing, perky, and giving, all to no avail, had finally dashed Janie's dreams. She was convinced that neither Mark nor the marriage had a pulse.

I'm tired. And I'm frustrated. But I'm also confused. Mark says that the problem is with me—that I expect too much out of marriage and out of him. He says he is the way that he is and "that can't be changed." I just need to accept him for who he is. Mark is perfectly happy with the way things have been. He firmly believes that if I'd just get my act together and stop trying to change things everything would be okay.

Is he right? Is there something wrong with me? Do I have the right to expect more from my marriage? Do I want too much? When Mark says, "This is the way that I am," should I accept that? Am I wrong in wanting him to be different—to behave in a way that suggests that he cares for me and our marriage? Should I just "accept things" and "be happy"? I don't know what's right or wrong anymore. I'm so confused!

## A Case of Confusion

Janie was asking some difficult questions. She was frustrated with her marriage. But she was also confused. In her mind, she was asking whether she even had the right to be unhappy. Should she not be content with what she had? Dare she desire more? Janie had given me a great deal of information. But had she given me enough to answer her questions?

The difficulty in answering questions like the ones Janie was asking is not so much with the amount of information you are given as with what you do with this information. Janie had given me events, behaviors, and frustrations. But how could I make sense out of these? How was I supposed to determine what was right and what was wrong between her and Mark? How was I supposed to differentiate the legitimate from the illegitimate, the healthy from the unhealthy, and the successful from the unsuccessful? Janie's questions were important. But her questions could not have been answered had I not already answered some that were even more important.

You always have to be concerned that information is accurate and realize that there are two perspectives in any marriage. But what enables you to understand confusing data is having your own set of personal beliefs about what constitutes marital health. You cannot begin to assess any problem, marital or otherwise, without first having a framework on which to base your evaluation. Without some underlying assumptions and beliefs (a standard), you have no means for giving order to otherwise chaotic bits of information. You too would be confused.

Janie's marriage made sense. Her descriptions of the events, the progressive deterioration, and her consequential myriad of emotions were perfectly understandable. But they only made sense because I had already answered the more important questions—the questions about what marriage is really all about. Once you have answered the big questions, answers to the little ones come easier.

## Making a Judgment Call

After more than twenty years of marriage, nearly as many years as a professional counselor, achieving two advanced degrees, and writing several books, time and experience have had an effect on my beliefs. For me, marriage and the pursuit of marital success have gradually been synthesized into three succinct and basic beliefs or premises. On these premises everything new that I learn, discover, or rediscover is cast and evaluated. And out of these premises everything that I say, write, or practice emerges. When it comes to marriage, this is what I believe.

### 1. I believe we are created for intimacy.

We are designed to be in intimate relationship. As Donald Joy states in the introduction to his book *Bonding: Relationships in the Image of God:*

> The basic thesis of this book is that *God's relationship with humans is one of intimate bonding, and that all human intimacies are "rehearsals" for the ultimate reunion of humans with their Creator.* Stated inversely, we might say that *all humans are bonding beings, such that their yearning for intimacy is an internal magnet which draws them, often unwittingly, toward God, for whose intimate relationship they are created.*[2]

I believe that Dr. Joy's understanding of our created complexity is accurate. We are created for intimacy—to be in intimate relationship with our Creator. Dr. Joy is echoing the fourth-century words of Augustine who wrote of the wandering that we are destined to do until we meet our God. It is only through finding God and filling the void in our lives that we find rest. The twentieth-century evangelistic organization, Campus Crusade for Christ, expressed the same truth when referring to the "God-shaped vacuum" in every person's heart that must be filled if he or she is to find peace. All attest to the reality of humans as bonding beings—creations who yearn to be in intimate relationship with their Creator.

But intimacy is our nature both *vertically* and *horizontally*—with God and with others. What we "createdly" yearn for vertically, we also "createdly" desire horizontally. The relationships that we experience horizontally, of which marriage is the most preeminent, are tangible representations of the spiritual (vertical) relationship that we experience with Christ. We are *companion beings* created to be in intimate relationship with others. Without this closeness, we are unfulfilled.

Family researchers argue that intimacy in marriage is far broader than one dimension. It is further argued that if a couple is to achieve a significant degree of closeness, it will not be the result of success in one dimension alone, regardless of the dimension, but will be the result of success in several areas. Six dimensions of intimacy are usually identified: emotional, intellectual, sexual, recreational, social, and spiritual. A true indication of intimacy is a combination of how a couple fares in all of these areas.

The development of intimacy determines whether a marriage is successful or not. How well are you bonding together? Are you achieving the level of intimacy for which you were created? Is closeness being developed in all the various dimensions that comprise the whole of intimacy? The degree to which intimacy is being achieved within a marriage determines the success or failure of that relationship.

*2. I believe marital success (and failure) is a process and not an event.*

It is the bottom line—the end result—that usually catches our attention. But most of the work, whether for good or for bad, occurs over time, and the results are always the product of many actions, not just one. This is how marriage works; it is a process, not an event. Whether successful or unsuccessful, it is the result of gradual movement involving many actions, not a lone event. The following story illustrates this point.

My secretary informed me that a long-distance caller was holding for me. In beginning our conversation, the caller informed me that he was a pastor and that he was "scared." When I inquired what he was afraid of, he replied, "I don't know." The pastor (I'll call him Doug) seemed a little reluctant to talk, so I began by inquiring about what was going on in his life. Something had to have occurred to cause the call. With a little encouragement, Doug began to tell me that he had just been given some startling information. A colleague, a close personal friend, had resigned his pastorate, left his wife and children, and begun living with another woman.

> I've had three pastorates during the past sixteen years. Most of them have been in this region of the United States, so I've gotten to know quite a few people. This is the fifth time during those sixteen years of ministry that someone I valued as a close personal friend, as well as a comrade in ministry, has done this.

It saddens me to see the pain that is associated with marital crisis, for both adults and children. And I am sometimes even angered by blatant acts of selfishness inflicted by mates on people they supposedly loved. But this never makes me *scared*. Why had it affected Doug in this manner?

"What are you afraid of?" I asked him.

"I'm afraid it might happen to me," he replied.

"Did you feel that way after the first time you witnessed a colleague and friend have an affair?"

"No."

"Did you feel that way after the second?"

"No."

"Then why do you feel scared now?"

"I don't know."

There is always a reason. Doug called me because of learning of his friend's actions and his own consequential emotional reaction. There was also a reason for his fear. He had experienced the same event on four previous occasions, but at none of those times had he been struck with fear. Why now? He said he didn't know. I suspected that he did. Even if he wasn't totally sure, Doug at least had some idea. He just didn't want to talk about it. So I began to follow my instinct and asked him to tell me about his marriage.

"What's it like?" I asked.

"Our marriage is stable but static—as are most of those around us. But we've been married for seventeen years. You don't expect it to be like it was when you first got married. Your marriage changes. We love each other, but we're busy. And there are a lot of pressures in the ministry," he replied.

"How much do you invest in your marriage?"

"I don't know. As I said, we're both pretty busy."

I don't like "I don't knows." They usually mean "I don't want to say" or "Don't press me on this." People know. For some reason, they just don't want to talk about it. Doug had given me three "I don't knows." I figured he had reached his limit.

"Describe for me a normal day," I said.

"Well, let me tell you about yesterday. I started off at 6:00 A.M. by having coffee with one of my laymen at the diner. By the time I finished with all of my responsibilities, I stumbled into the house somewhere around midnight. Now, that's not a *normal* day, but it's not all that uncommon, either," he replied.

Doug was a successful pastor. But as he continued to describe his all-too-hectic lifestyle, I was reminded of another pastor who had called in utter frustration and reported, "I'm 'more than a conqueror' in every area of my life . . . every area, that is, except my marriage." From Doug's description, it would be a fair assumption that there wasn't much being invested in his marriage. I think he already knew that. It was probably his recognition of the consequences of failing to invest in his marriage that had scared him so. My guess was that, at least relationally, there wasn't much there. So I began to give him a little feedback.

"Doug, you're a pastor," I said. "Let me give you a spiritual metaphor. What would you do if a church member came to you and said: 'My relationship with the Lord is stable but static, as is the case with most of those around me. But I've been a Christian for seventeen years. You don't expect it to be like it was when you first were converted. Your relationship changes. I love the Lord, but I'm pretty busy. And there are a lot of demands on my life.'

"What would be your position with your church members, Doug? They all have static spiritual relationships. But 'things change. What do you expect after seventeen years?' Would you be satisfied with this position? Or would you say, 'Hold it a minute. Something isn't right here!'

"My guess is that it would be the latter. You would probably try and schedule a revival. Sure, our relationship with the Lord changes. But it should be changing for the better. It ought to be growing deeper and more intimate, not becoming static.

"Well, *marriage is the same way.*"

Doug's marriage had been failing, but its failure had not been obvious. Doug and his wife were in the "ideal couple" syndrome. Their marriage looked fine from the outside. When together they were cordial, friendly, and active. Their marriage also worked pretty well on the inside. It was functionally satisfactory. They were co-operative. Dual careers, church responsibilities, the raising of children—all of the essential tasks were being handled. But their marriage was actually dying.

Doug's marriage was void of emotion. Both he and his wife were anesthetized to feelings. There were no negatives causing disruption, but neither were there any positives bonding them together. They were just drifting along in a lifeless, non-intimate, and emotionally distant relationship. Their marriage was failing. But this failure had not come as an event; it had been progressive. Action upon action and decision upon decision—each robbing the marriage of needed time and prioritization—had taken a gradual but deadly toll. It may be that an *event* will bring their relationship to a point of crisis, but a *process* had already brought it to failure. That is the way it is with all marriages. Success or failure is through process.

*3. I believe we can desire an intimate relationship but unless we are willing to deal with the interferences to marital growth, we will not likely achieve it.*

Desire, knowledge, understanding—these are all important if we are to grow in our marriages. But these alone will not get the job done. A successful marriage will require more than good intentions.

It will require fortitude, follow-through, and the tenacity to face any obstacle—anything that would stand in the way of reaching your goal.

In every marriage, there are things that will interfere with the easy achievement of intimacy. The interferences that plague a relationship are as idiosyncratic as the partners themselves. It may be simply the need to prioritize your life by placing your marriage above other pressing but less significant matters—dodging the temptation of dealing with the urgent instead of the truly important. But for most of us, more items can be added to our interference list.

Avoidance tendencies, whether relating to dissatisfactions or self-disclosure, can be placed high on the interference list. They are high both in frequency and consequence. It may be that you've never learned to deal with anger, so it creates difficulty in your marriage. It may be that you have tendencies toward insensitivity that block closeness and damage your mate's self-esteem. Or it may be that the lack of a genuine commitment—doing what is in the best interest of the relationship as opposed to what is most comfortable—stands in your way. Regardless of the form in which interference comes to your marriage, you must be willing to actively confront it. Otherwise, intimacy will elude you.

## Back to Janie and Mark

Remember Janie? She was frustrated and unhappy. But she was also confused. Do you remember her questions? "Is there something wrong with me? Am I expecting too much? When Mark says, 'This is the way that I am,' should I accept that?" Based on what you know about Janie's marriage, and in view of my basic premises for marital health, what do you think my assessment would be?

Janie had a right to be frustrated. I did not see anything wrong with her expectations of marriage. She desired an intimate relationship. This was a healthy desire, but one that she had failed to achieve. She and Mark had an arrangement, not a companionship. And this was far less than what they could and should have had. Was Mark correct in saying, "This is the way that I am"? Mark's assessment of himself was accurate. But his assumptions of license, justification, and either being unable to or not needing to change were erroneous. His being who he was was interfering with the marriage moving in a healthy direction. Unless he were to deal with himself, things would not likely improve. Sure, Janie could accept that things would continue as they were. And if she were able to emotionally disengage from her marriage, she might even find a little contentment. But would this really be a marriage? The institution may continue intact, but the relationship would die. It would continue to be an arrangement—and a failure.

According to my first premise, marital success or failure is dependent upon the achievement of intimacy in the marriage. Were Mark and Janie moving in a bonding direction? No. According to my second premise, marital success or failure is a process and not an event. Mark and Janie's marriage aptly illustrated the process nature of failure. Their failure was the result of twenty years of process—twenty years of Mark withholding himself and investing out of the marriage and Janie trying to make everything right. They were prime for a crisis. And according to my final premise, marital success requires more than desire and good intentions. It requires two mates who are willing to face and resolve the idiosyncratic interferences that exist in their relationship. This Mark also refused to do. His solution was for Janie to accept him as he was and allow him to continue to be emotionally closed, distant, and peripheral to the marriage. This was hardly a solution that would bring intimacy.

Janie was frustrated. She had every right to be. Together, we would attempt to deal with her level of frustration. And we would also deal with some changes in Janie's behavior—changes that would be healthier for her individually and that might also influence Mark's behavior. But whether their marriage would reach a point of crisis or move toward a greater level of intimacy would largely depend on decisions made by Mark. He would have to choose to deal with his interferences. Otherwise, things would continue as they had been—failing.

*I Love You—Talk to Me!* emanates from my basic premises about marriage. I believe in its message. I stress that marital success is measured by the level of closeness we are able to establish in our relationtionship. Movement toward intimacy or disengagement is a process—a process that is the result of many actions, many themes, and a great deal of time. If an intimate relationship is achieved at all, it will come as the result of intentional effort—dealing with anything that may act as an interference. The particular interferences identified in this book are our natural tendencies to be avoidant. Though there are others, I know of none that are so generalizable. Avoidance is truly something with which we all must contend.

# Two

# 2

# Avoiding Conflict

# 5

# Deal with Me

The Thompsons and the Petersons were both couples with whom I counseled. Comparatively, there were many differences between these two marriages. For instance, the Thompsons were well educated, both having achieved advanced degrees; formal education for the Petersons ceased with their graduation from high school. Both Mr. and Mrs. Thompson had professional careers; Mr. Peterson worked as a laborer and Mrs. Peterson stayed at home with the youngest of their children. The Thompsons' children attended private school; the Petersons' attended public.

But the differences between these two couples extended beyond socioeconomic distinctions. Within their respective marriages, there was also a difference in how these mates related to one another. When dissatisfactions regarding his wife would arise, Mr. Thompson would simply dismiss them. He reasoned, "Why let the little things in life get you down? Just let them go and move on." When dissatisfactions would arise for Mr. Peterson, he found it more difficult to just let the little things go. Instead, he would get upset, sulk, refuse to talk for days at a time, and sometimes dramatically storm out of the house.

The differences between these two couples were so immense that it would be difficult for some to find any similarities at all. However, there was something they did share in common—the tendency to

avoid conflict. The Thompsons and the Petersons may have practiced avoidant behavior in different ways, but the end result was the
same—both of these marriages were avoidant.

In healthy marriages, mates deal with each other regarding dissatisfactions. They do not avoid. The cry of many partners in relationships similar to those just described is *deal with me.* Responding to this cry—to deal with conflict within marriage—requires that
each mate act according to the following definition: *to deal directly,
honestly, and appropriately with dissatisfaction in the relationship.*

To help determine whether a mate is truly dealing with dissatisfactions in a marriage, I gather responses to the following statements
in my marital interaction and communication inventory: "When
hurt or frustrated by something my mate has done, I tell him/her
honestly how I feel" and "I deal directly with my mate regarding con-
flictual issues. If not at the time of the conflict, then at least a little
later, after the problem has been given some thought."

Favorable responses (strong agreement with these statements)
suggest a tendency to deal in a healthy way with dissatisfactions as
they arise in the marriage. Less favorable responses (lack of agreement with these statements) suggest that avoidance may be a problem area in a relationship.

Whereas healthy behavior requires being direct, emotionally honest, and appropriate, avoidant behavior merely requires a failure to
be either direct, emotionally honest, or appropriate. To violate any
part of the definition of relational health is to violate the whole. Mr.
Thompson's manner of violating this definition may have been very
different from Mr. Peterson's, but both husbands were guilty of conflict avoidant behavior. And both marriages suffered the consequences of their avoidance.

## The Whats of Avoidance

When we speak of how a mate acts out his avoidance in a marriage, we are addressing the whats—*what* he is doing or *what* he is
not doing. So in describing what a mate does as an attempt to avoid
dealing with dissatisfactions, we are articulating the specific behav-

iors and actions he uses to achieve this end. The whats of avoidance—how it is actually accomplished—are behavioral in nature.

As was illustrated by the Thompsons and Petersons, there are many ways to be avoidant. Mr. Thompson's variation of avoidant behavior was far less noticeable than Mr. Peterson's. The dissatisfaction, and its ultimate dismissal, was totally confined to Mr. Thompson's thought processes. Once he mentally resolved a problem, he proceeded as if nothing had ever happened. His wife was none the wiser. Much to the contrary, there was no subtlety to Mr. Peterson's behavior regarding his dissatisfaction. His abrupt actions easily allowed his wife to be aware that something was not right. Yet even though he made his displeasure known, he made no attempt to deal directly with the problem. In both cases, an avoidant scenario was acted out.

A significant part of releasing the grip that avoidance may have on a relationship lies in determining the whats. How is conflict avoidance played out in your relationship? Who does what? In the remainder of this chapter, I will describe the behavioral variations that are most commonly presented in counseling. See if any are applicable to your marriage.

## Stuffing

*Stuffing* (suppressing feelings) is a visually descriptive term. It carries the implication that space is being filled up—which is exactly what happens when stuffing occurs as a pattern in a relationship. Whenever a dissatisfaction is stuffed instead of being expressed and resolved, a residual emotion stays inside. With each additional instance, the residue increases. It is not difficult to picture how the long-term utilization of such a tactic can lead to bitterness.

I assess a mate's tendency to stuff by gaining either agreement or disagreement to the following statement: "I 'keep it to myself' when I'm mad at my spouse." At the very least, stuffing represents emotional dishonesty. Rather than sharing what is actually felt or believed (the truth), a tactic is taken that misrepresents the truth.

The goal of this behavior is to *fool others*. The truth is clearly known to the dissatisfied and avoidant spouse. He admits to himself that he is unhappy, or upset, or hurt. But this knowledge is intentionally withheld from his mate, a clear act of deception. He may have an occasional and episodic emotional outburst. Like a boiler that reaches its maximum capacity, an emotional safety valve allows the release of some excess steam. In some degree of awe, a confused spouse may respond to the unanticipated eruption with a series of questions: "What has gotten into you? What is it that I said?" But when composure is regained, the marriage will proceed with the avoidant mate continuing to stuff his real feelings.

A marriage of this type continues in a state of pretense as if nothing were the matter. But with the avoidant mate being fully aware of his displeasure, it is only a matter of time before reality—the truth in the relationship—emerges.

### Ignoring

Ignoring dissatisfactions has many similarities to stuffing. For instance, it is also an example of emotional dishonesty. The truth is known, but what is real and true regarding the relationship is not expressed. Instead of dealing honestly and directly with whatever the dissatisfaction may be, the truth is deceptively withheld from the unsuspecting mate. Stuffing and ignoring also share the tendency to be misleading. But rather than fooling others, the avoidant mate is attempting to *fool himself.*

With stuffing, there is no denial that the spouse is unhappy. He just doesn't want others to know of his displeasure, so he stuffs it. With ignoring, however, the reality of the displeasure is gradually brought into question by the mate himself: "Why did I get upset about that? It is such a little thing. It doesn't really matter anyway." Ultimately, this highly sophisticated means of mental maneuvering results in the problem either being dismissed as insignificant or forgotten altogether. With either action, no further attention to the problem is required. After all, if there is no problem—if the displeasure can be discounted or erased—there is nothing that needs to be either confronted or addressed.

Mr. Thompson illustrated this practice. He would become upset with something that his wife either did or did not do. But he quickly rationalized her behavior and his feelings regarding her behavior to eliminate any necessity to deal with her. After all, if no problem exists, there is nothing with which to contend.

Ignoring is an attempt at denial. In essence it rewrites history. You convince yourself that what you thought occurred really didn't. The incident was only an illusion. Or, if it did occur, its significance wasn't really as important as first thought: "It doesn't really matter." With both attempts the same goal is reached—avoidance.

I assess a mate's tendency to ignore dissatisfactions by gaining either agreement or disagreement to this statement: "Though truly irritated by something that my mate says or does, I usually just dismiss it and forget it happened." Mates who agree with this statement are likely to pretend that nothing is the matter. A therapist colleague has repeatedly made the statement, "Reality's what is." What she means is regardless of how much I may choose to deny, pretend, dismiss, or just forget, nothing changes what is real. And reality always finds a way of making its presence known.

## Dealing Indirectly

When marital dissatisfaction is handled in an indirect manner, there is no question in either partner's mind that one of the mates is displeased. Though the fact may not be immediately known by the other mate, the secret will not be kept for long. Soon both will be painfully aware that all is not well.

You may be asking yourself the question, "If it is inappropriate to keep dissatisfaction to yourself, and dealing indirectly with displeasures eventually results in a mate's realization that there is dissatisfaction, why is this tactic being presented in such a negative light?" As we will see, some of the problems with indirectness are the specific behaviors themselves, which are in many ways quite inappropriate. However, an even greater problem is the *goal* of these behaviors. The ultimate goal of genuinely dealing with dissatisfaction is to bring resolution to the problem; it is constructive. Indirectness has no such goal. When dealing indirectly with marital dissatisfaction, the disgruntled spouse has only one aim—retaliation. He has been hurt and now he is responding in like fashion. The goal is to inflict pain and disruption, a far cry from resolution.

An old saying captures the essence of indirectness: "If mama ain't happy, ain't nobody happy." In other words, if one person is displeased, he or she finds a way to not only insure that everyone else becomes aware of the displeasure, but that they also share in the discomfort as much as possible. As you may recall, this was the practice illustrated by Mr. Peterson. He made certain that his wife was aware of his displeasure. But he made no attempt to resolve his dissatisfaction. He was content to vent.

I assess a mate's tendency to deal indirectly with dissatisfactions by gaining either agreement or disagreement to the following statement: "Though I don't deal directly with my mate about being angry, he/she 'gets the message' through other things that I do (i.e., I get quiet, uncooperative, emotionally distant, etc.)." A mate who tends to agree with this statement finds a way to get across the message, "I am not a happy camper." Unfortunately for both the message sender and the message receiver, the indirect means of expression hinders the potential for healthy resolution of the displeasure. As one wife stated, "I let Jim know that I am upset 'in other ways.'" This mate, and many others like her, are not guilty of totally failing to deal with their dissatisfactions. There is no denial. At least to some extent, they are admitting to themselves and expressing to others that they are displeased. But the indirect manner of handling their dissatisfaction only creates further tension in the marriage.

A classic example of dealing indirectly with dissatisfactions is to throw "zingers" at a mate. Similar to sniper fire in guerrilla warfare, these unsuspecting comments catch you totally off guard. You ask yourself, "What was that about?" With zingers, it may not be the words that strike the nerve, but the tone in which the message is delivered. "No. I don't mind if you take a nap while I straighten up the house. I'll try to work quietly so as not to disturb your sleep." The words look innocent enough on paper. But verbal tone can change the connotative meaning significantly. If this is a zinger, the nap will not be nearly as restful as hoped.

Other forms of indirect dealings will probably be as familiar as zingers. For instance, no matter how kind the words, if they are accompanied by tightly gritted teeth and a plastic smile, the facial expression will convey more meaning than the words. Then there is the old tactic of feigned denial—"Wrong? What makes you think anything is wrong?"—accompanied by the slamming of a door or the view of a mate's back as he ceremonially storms out of the room. The silent treatment (cold shoulder), the withdrawal of affection, a rigid body posture whenever you draw near . . . as this list attests, there are many ways to indirectly deal with dissatisfaction.

Unlike stuffing and ignoring, in indirect dealings the message of displeasure is sounded out loud and clear. But awareness only results in more tension for the couple and does not seem to enhance their potential for resolving the problem. Dealing with the particular dissatisfaction is as soundly avoided as if it had been stuffed or ignored. As a result, the marriage ultimately experiences the same consequence.

### Physical Withdrawal

Physically withdrawing from the proximity of your spouse when you are displeased can be accomplished with or without your mate's becoming aware of your displeasure. Awareness of displeasure is largely dependent on the amount of fanfare associated with the departure. If your intent is to maintain secrecy, your behavior is simply emotionally dishonest. If on the other hand you desire for your mate to be aware of your dissatisfaction but have no intent of dealing with the difficulty, withdrawing from the scene is much like the indirect tactics discussed in the last section.

I assess a mate's tendency to physically withdraw when dissatisfied by gaining either agreement or disagreement to the following statement: "When truly angry with my mate, I leave the room." A mate who tends to agree with this statement seeks to avoid conflict by getting the source of his displeasure away from him, though it is he who actually does the relocating. The premise that is being followed is this, "If you're not there, you can't deal."

Sometimes the avoidant mate is attempting to get "out of the line of fire." It is not he who is displeased but his spouse. However, regardless of who is dissatisfied, his desire to avoid any form of confrontation prompts his relocation. The withdrawing mate may think that a little time apart will allow him the opportunity to cool off. He thinks, "Given a little time to myself, I'll be able to rationalize my dissatisfaction away." In either case, the withdrawal will be subtle or camouflaged. A mate will quietly leave the room or find an excuse to make a trip to the store. I have known some mates who have adopted this tactic as a complete lifestyle as opposed to a merely episodic reaction. They spend large amounts of time away from home, frequently investing their energy in worthy endeavors. These mates are sometimes mislabeled as workaholics. Though there are men and women who correctly deserve the title of workaholic, the distinguishing characteristic that differentiates between these similar forms of behavior is motivation. Withdrawing mates are not driven men and women who must achieve. Avoidant mates like these throw themselves into outside interests in an effort to avoid conflict at home.

If the withdrawing behavior is intended to also convey an indirect message of dissatisfaction, the departure will be more dramatic. There will be a final word spoken, or an abruptness to the departure, or a heavy sigh, or a slammed door. Something will be done to bring awareness but not resolution.

Whether with the singular intent of emotional dishonesty or with the added flavor of indirectness, there is something poignantly symbolic in one who physically withdraws from a mate. As the behavior is reenacted, he may find himself doing more than momentarily changing his location—he may find that walking away from conflicts results in his walking away from his marriage. Every journey begins with an initial step.

### Overreacting

When a mate overreacts, the hurt, disappointment, or frustration that has created his dissatisfaction and accompanying anger is expressed in an excessive and extreme manner. This excessiveness may be limited to a verbal barrage and a harshness in tone. Or it may move in an ascending order of intensity with the dissatisfied mate making demeaning or intimidating statements. The addition of threats represents an even greater escalation, and a proverbial line is crossed whenever the actions move from being purely verbal to including more physical expressions (throwing or breaking objects or touching or hitting a spouse).

Overreactions of this nature have far-reaching and destructive consequences for a marriage. If this is a pattern, especially in the case of physical or violent reactions, professional assistance should be sought immediately. There is a clear indication of anger and impulse control difficulties in the overreacting spouse. Overreactions can also be a means of avoidance.

I assess a mate's tendency to overreact to marital dissatisfaction by gaining either agreement or disagreement to the following statement: "When angry with my mate, I tend to get upset and 'blow up' at him/her." Overreactive behavior is not emotional dishonesty. There is no mistaking the mate's attitude—he is upset. Neither is this behavior necessarily indirect; the displeasure is clearly stated, so it would be difficult to say that it violates the "directness" quality of our definition of health stated at the beginning of this chapter. It could be argued that this form of behavior lacks the clear goal of mutual resolution because the dissatisfied mate aims to "resolve" the difficulty by winning. However, what we can most assuredly state is that this form of behavior is inappropriate. It seeks to dominate, to suppress, and to squelch any form of resistance. Stated briefly, it seeks to avoid dealing (genuinely dealing) with any relational dissatisfaction by overpowering the opposition. The other mate, after being confronted by such a display of force, is expected to surrender. From the vantage point of the dissatisfied mate, his dissatisfaction has been expressed, dealt with, and is now resolved. His mate has succumbed to his pressure.

But this is not resolution—it is avoidance. Dissatisfactions have been identified and words have been spoken. But the words have been harsh words, and the goal has not been to deal. In fact, the real goal was to avoid dealing—to avoid talking, expressing, sharing, and mutually resolving. If there is an appearance of resolution, it is probably the result of fear or resignation on the part of the overpowered and intimidated spouse. The "what's the use" attitude becomes pervasive.

Though each of the avoidance strategies has the potential to lead a marriage toward a state of crisis, there is none more destructive in nature than overreacting. It allows for the development of so many unhealthy characteristics from bitterness to a loss of hope. It is truly a characteristic that must be confronted and changed.

# Reflecting on Conflict Avoidance

This chapter sought to define what constitutes the healthy handling of marital dissatisfactions. It also described the natural tendencies that interfere with accomplishing this goal. Five common avoidance tendencies were identified. The rating scale listed below has been included to help you identify possible areas of difficulty within your own marriage. When dissatisfied with something your mate has done, how frequently do you utilize each of these behaviors? Two scales are provided offering an opportunity for both partners to respond. Place a mark on the appropriate scale indicating your typical behavior.

• Stuffing: "I keep it to myself."

| **Husband** | **Wife** |
|---|---|
| ☐ Never | ☐ Never |
| ☐ Occasionally | ☐ Occasionally |
| ☐ Commonly | ☐ Commonly |
| ☐ Frequently | ☐ Frequently |
| ☐ Always | ☐ Always |

• Ignoring: "I usually dismiss it and forget it ever happened."

| **Husband** | **Wife** |
|---|---|
| ☐ Never | ☐ Never |
| ☐ Occasionally | ☐ Occasionally |
| ☐ Commonly | ☐ Commonly |
| ☐ Frequently | ☐ Frequently |
| ☐ Always | ☐ Always |

• Dealing Indirectly: "My mate gets the message through 'other things' that I do."

| Husband | Wife |
|---|---|
| ☐ Never | ☐ Never |
| ☐ Occasionally | ☐ Occasionally |
| ☐ Commonly | ☐ Commonly |
| ☐ Frequently | ☐ Frequently |
| ☐ Always | ☐ Always |

• Physical Withdrawal: "I leave the room."

| Husband | Wife |
|---|---|
| ☐ Never | ☐ Never |
| ☐ Occasionally | ☐ Occasionally |
| ☐ Commonly | ☐ Commonly |
| ☐ Frequently | ☐ Frequently |
| ☐ Always | ☐ Always |

• Overreacting: "I 'blow up' when dissatisfied."

| Husband | Wife |
|---|---|
| ☐ Never | ☐ Never |
| ☐ Occasionally | ☐ Occasionally |
| ☐ Commonly | ☐ Commonly |
| ☐ Frequently | ☐ Frequently |
| ☐ Always | ☐ Always |

# 6

# Blocking and Pushing

Marriage is designed to be an intimate relationship. Saying "I do" *begins* this process. It is not the culmination or *end*. With the passage of time, husbands and wives will face a multitude of events together. Some of these will be viewed as good; others will be labeled interruptions, misfortunes, and tragedies. There will be times of disagreement when mates just do not see eye-to-eye. And there will be times of disappointment when either through intent, accident, or misinterpretation, a spouse judges a mate's behavior to be inappropriate. Ideally, these events and times of life will provide opportunities for mates to draw closer together, to form a more united union. This is the hope, if not always the result.

Many things emerge that interfere with the process of growing together. Some of these interferences are subtle; others are obvious. Some are pathological; others are normal. Over the course of several years as a marital therapist, I have found no tendency more deserving of the title of interference to the process of healthy marital growth than avoiding to deal with dissatisfactions.

Conflict avoidance totally undermines a couple's progress toward closeness. In some relationships, this undermining takes the form of an emotional *block* toward their otherwise desired level of intimacy. In other relationships, the mates are actually *pushed* apart. Though different in quality and intensity, I generally find that these two problems occur in a progression; one seems to precede the other. And both—being *blocked* or *pushed*—are dynamic or interactive. As we will now discover, each in its own way actively frustrates a couple's true desire for closeness.

## Blocks, Walls, and Other Obstacles

Being blocked in a relationship is the result of failing to deal with simple anger. The natural by-product of relational dissatisfactions is anger. It is the normal human response to being either hurt or frustrated. Failing to deal with the particular dissatisfaction—being conflict avoidant—eliminates the opportunity for a couple to resolve this anger in a healthy way. The principle is simple—if you do not deal, you cannot settle. The immediate consequence of this avoidant behavior for the marriage is seen in the couple's level of closeness. Any movement toward one another in an attempt to be emotionally close is *blocked*.

The relationship principle that operates here is easily recognizable. It is difficult to emotionally move toward and draw close to someone who has hurt you or with whom you are angry. Conversely, it is equally difficult to allow this person to draw close to you. In times like these, it is not closeness that you desire but distance. When emotional issues are allowed to continue unattended and unresolved, you might as well erect a physical wall in the marriage. It will be no less an obstacle to overcome than the emotional wall.

There has been a great deal of discussion recently regarding the establishment of healthy *boundaries* in a person's life. These personally established benchmarks help us to know where our responsibilities end and another's begin whether related to our activities or our relationships. Appropriate boundaries are necessary for both personal and relational well-being. Walls, however, are a far different matter.

Walls are barriers, obstacles intentionally erected to serve as an obstruction. Like the fences in our yards, they are meant to accomplish far more than simply identify the property line. They are erected to keep people away. The relational walls that are erected as a consequence of failing to resolve dissatisfactions have the same goal: They are erected to separate us.

It was Sunday afternoon. Church services had been good that morning and so had lunch. My wife, Jan, and I were now at home relaxing. Sunday afternoon seems to be the one time during the week when relaxation is the expectation and not the exception. Things were quiet in the house but that had not struck me as unusual. After all, it was Sunday.

Jan had been busying herself with various activities and I had been doing the same. But as the afternoon progressed, I began to detect a less than nurturing tone in the few statements that Jan did direct my way. After one curt exchange, I asked if she was angry with me. Jan stopped what she was doing and stood motionless. This was not a stance of fear, "Oh no, I have been caught"; her hesitation was more pensive. Finally, she answered, "Yes. I guess I am." My response required no contemplation. "Well, I would rather that you deal with me if you're angry than to throw zingers at me all afternoon." Jan's retort was classic and representative of the differences in both our personalities and the situations in which we had been raised. "It just takes me a little longer to figure out I'm angry than it does you."

Jan was being honest in her assessment of being slow to anger— or at least in being slow to recognize her anger. She was raised in a conservative Christian home, one with a multiple-generation history in the same denomination, in the South. This Christian culture valued being nice to everyone (always) and devalued getting angry (ever). Though Jan is still nice to everyone, her travels through the years of adulthood have brought her the realization that what is sometimes presented as religiously appropriate is not always scripturally correct nor emotionally healthy. She has learned that anger in and of itself is not sinful but actually normal. However, old patterns can be tenacious, so when Jan stated, "It just takes me a little longer to figure out I'm angry than it does you," she was accurately reporting what takes place in her. She has to do a little processing.

I, on the other hand, was raised in a non-Christian, non-Southern environment and was not exposed to the conservative admonition that anger is sinful. Consequently, I experience far fewer hesitations and "do anger" real well.

With the dissatisfaction brought to the forefront, Jan and I were able to address the difficulty. However, we could have chosen to do otherwise. Jan could have opted for denial. "Angry? No, I'm not angry. Whatever gave you that idea?" I could have withdrawn from the confrontation hoping that time would be a cure-all for whatever was bothering her. But avoidance was not the choice either of us made. What followed was an attempt by both of us to deal with Jan's dissatisfaction.

There were a few tense moments, but in relatively quick fashion we were able to resolve the problem. This resolution brought two changes in our relationship. First was a feeling of emotional relief. The intensity of emotion that Jan had been experiencing dissipated—she was no longer angry with me. Instead, feelings of a much more positive nature were allowed to return. Second was a freeing of movement. Prior to dealing with the dissatisfaction, Jan was distant. Her relational movement was blocked by her anger. Whether for fear of further hurt or merely a lack of desire to be close, Jan had insulated herself within our relationship with a wall. Now we were again free to move toward one another. She no longer felt a need to maintain any distance—to pull back. Nor did she feel a need to block me should I attempt to move toward her.

Jan did not hate me. She was not resentful. She was simply angry. This created distance in our relationship. Had we failed to deal with her dissatisfaction and resolve the anger, not only would the block in our relationship have been maintained, but the consequence of this failure to deal could have led to an even greater problem.

## Pushing Apart

One of the saddest examples of marital deterioration was shared with me by a woman who had been married for more than forty years.

I met Richard when I was seventeen and he was twenty. I had finished high school early and was already living on my own and supporting myself. I was working as a bookkeeper for a small manufacturer. It was a responsible job for someone as young as I was—but I had always been responsible. Maybe *too* responsible.

I had been dating another boy for a couple of years. He wasn't from my town but spent his summers there because it was a resort area. John was from a wealthy family, and they always took summers off. He was in college, and we would write during the fall and spring semesters. We had talked about getting married. Not seriously, but enough for us both to believe that marriage was probably where our relationship was going to end up. Then Richard entered my life.

Richard appeared out of nowhere. And when he did, my previously sensible, ordered, and well-planned existence was totally disrupted. Richard was different from all of the other boys I had dated. He was so nice to me. But he was also exciting. He really knew how to have a good time. Richard had a good job working for his brother when we met, and I just assumed he was a responsible sort of person. At the end of the summer, John returned home and then back to college. We continued to write for a brief period of time, but that stopped as Richard and I began seeing more of each other. I really felt something special for Richard. We were married by Christmas. (Linda's voice grew softer and she looked away.) We were so much in love back then.

The time that Linda had just described was a glimpse of her past—a time from which she was now far removed. Things were simpler then. At least, that was how they appeared. Now they were more complex. Linda sat in my office because Richard, the one for whom she had felt "something special" over forty years earlier, had left her. There had been no warning. Linda suspected nothing. From her perspective, Richard left her life just as abruptly as he entered it.

I didn't see it coming. Maybe I should have. Things had not been good between us for a long time. I knew it and I suspected Richard did as well—though he never talked about being unhappy. That was typical for Richard. He was always pleasant—never one to talk about what he felt whether it was negative or positive. Communicating with Richard was like playing twenty questions. I always had to pry answers out of him. So I only assumed he wasn't happy because I wasn't happy.

Things hadn't been good. I'll admit that. But for Richard to just up and leave . . . I don't know. (Linda paused and then donned a quizzical expression.) Why? Richard wasn't *saying* anything that he hadn't said for the last forty years. He wasn't complaining. He wasn't grouchy. And he wasn't *doing* anything any differently. He wasn't staying out late. He wasn't running around with anybody else. On the last day that we spent together, do you know what his parting words were to me as we both left for work? "I'll see you when you get home this evening." (Another pause.) That never happened.

When I walked into the house that evening, I knew something was wrong. There was no Richard, but that wasn't what clued me in. It was that everything that was *his* was gone. A surgeon couldn't have cut through the house any cleaner. Where two pictures had been on the wall, only one remained. A small table that had belonged to his parents and had stood in our dining room for years was no longer there. The lamp and flowers that had sat on it were placed neatly on the floor—exactly where the table had stood and in the exact same arrangement. Everything was the same minus the table. The whole house was that way. It was eerie.

I was stunned—in total shock. I couldn't believe this had happened. I wasn't even sure what *had* happened! Well, that was eight months ago. It was three months before I even had any contact with Richard. And then, it was only because I was able to track him down. It was as if he had dropped off the end of the earth. It's eight months later, and I still don't know much more now than I did when he left. I'm still confused. And I still can't get him to talk to me. I just need to figure out what to do with my life.

Linda's marriage (specifically) and her life (in general) were both in a state of chaos. Though our initial focus would be to bring some sort of order back into her otherwise chaotic existence, there was no guarantee in what form this stability might appear—whether order would return with the reconciliation of her marriage or whether it would ultimately return with its dissolution. As we sat and talked, my thoughts kept gravitating to questions. Linda and Richard had spent over forty years of their lives together. Forty years! What happened? What led them to this place? What was their marital history?

I knew that the future is not controlled by the past, but I also knew that evaluating the history of their marriage could bring some understanding of present events and possibly influence what we chose to do. What were the themes in their marriage? When did things begin to deteriorate?

Linda related a history that became sadder with each phrase. There were times of tenderness and love—the demonstrations of genuine caring. But these were largely confined to the early years. With the passage of time, these demonstrations became fewer and fewer. A void gradually crept into the marriage. The change seemed to be ushered in by actions best described as irresponsible and avoidant.

Linda said she entered marriage with youthful idealism. She envisioned that she and Richard would start a family and that she would raise their children in a small but adequate house surrounded by a white picket fence. She would be at home to care for the children— he would work to support the family. Everyone would be happy. Was that too much to expect? Linda had come from a poor and unstable background. Though she did not desire affluence, she did desire stability, which had been absent in her childhood. However, it would prove to be something that would also elude her in marriage.

> Richard had over fifty jobs during our forty-two years together. The grass always seemed to be greener somewhere else. I didn't realize what was going on in the beginning. Richard would be working somewhere and then, all of a sudden, he wasn't going to work anymore. There was always some reason—the boss wasn't good, the job didn't have a future, or he was going to make it big doing something else somewhere else.
>
> Sometimes Richard wouldn't tell me he was out of work. I'd find out when we got evicted or when the electricity was cut off. We moved a lot. Sometimes within the same city but frequently to another state. There was always something or someplace that was going to be a better opportunity.
>
> Richard was always promising to make it big—things would be better. After five years of this crisis-to-crisis existence, I realized that if any stability was going to come to our family life, it was going to come because of what I did and not Richard. So I went back to work.

Returning to work marked the loss of another part of Linda's dream. Their constant moving about had struck hard at the white picket fence idea. Now, instead of being at home with her children, she was waiting on customers. "Somebody had to do something." But probably the greatest blow to Linda's dream came with a changed perspective of Richard. Linda began to resign herself to a previously resisted reality—she was not going to be able to rely on her husband.

Linda's growing disappointment in Richard and her frustration with their chaotic lifestyle did little to change Richard's behavior. Attempts to talk to him regarding her dissatisfactions proved futile. He would not deal. Linda's willingness to try to deal with Richard began to wane. Her attempts to resolve her marital dissatisfactions grew more and more infrequent. The years passed and their nomadic lifestyle continued. There were more jobs, more moves, and more disappointments.

The void between Linda and Richard continued to grow. From all appearances, Richard was content to have a superficial relationship. Linda felt the need for communication that would bring resolution, but this was not to occur. The children grew up and left home. Only she and Richard remained. They were in the Midwest when Richard was again out of work and suggested another move. This time, he wanted to relocate in the South. After several years of working in unrelated jobs, Linda had found employment with a national concern. Rather than starting over with each move, she had been able to negotiate transfers. When Richard decided it was time to move south, Linda initiated another transfer request. The transfer was approved, and she and Richard headed toward another fresh start. It was en route to this next in a long list of new beginnings that a pivotal change in their relationship occurred.

We were driving south. It was a long trip, so Richard was a captive audience. I remember telling myself, "Richard doesn't have to talk to me, but he at least has to listen." I hoped for more. I hoped for change. I wanted to be surprised. I wanted Richard to actually talk to me—to listen to what I was feeling and to give me some assurance that our lives and marriage would be different. But he didn't. He was silent for the entire trip.

I thought I was going to be okay with Richard's silence. But I guess I wasn't. When we got to where we were going, I told him I was moving into one bedroom, and he could move into the other. We could resume sleeping together when he was willing to start communicating with me. I wasn't trying to punish him. I was just tired of things being the way they were. Maybe that was the wrong thing for me to do. But I didn't know of any other alternatives. We lived that way for eight years—until the day I came home to find Richard was gone.

During those eight years, Richard's behavior never changed. He had several jobs. None seemed to suit him or to be good enough. He continued to treat Linda pleasantly. From time to time, he would suggest that they sleep together. But when she refused, he did not get terribly upset. Linda would reiterate her need for him to be willing to deal with her before anything else would change. But it made no difference. Richard continued to resist. They went through the motions of maintaining a household, but there was no intimacy in the marriage on any dimension. There was only void.

My thesis is that couples who do not deal with the dissatisfactions that naturally arise within marriage begin by building walls. But if their avoidant behavior is still not corrected, they progress to a full-blown resentment. Following my thesis, I asked Linda when she began to feel resentful toward Richard. My question was met with silence. In part, the question was unexpected. After all, Linda was here to talk about her present confusion and the rotten thing that Richard had done to her. She did not come intending to discuss the resentment that had developed within her over the course of several years of failing to resolve dissatisfactions. But after giving it some thought, Linda responded to my inquiry.

I hadn't really thought of myself as growing resentful. But I guess I had. There were so many dreams dashed, so many hurts, and so many disappointments. I probably began resenting Richard when I realized it was never going to be any different—that he wasn't going to be reliable and, no matter what I did, he just wasn't going to communicate with me.

I guess these realizations began in the first ten years of our marriage. I think I began to *push* him away after that—to keep my distance.

"What about Richard? When did he become resentful?" This was also a difficult question for Linda. After all, Richard had always been pleasant toward her. She could not see where he had evidenced any signs of resentment. "Of course, there was the letter that he left behind when he walked out of my life eight months ago." This was the first I had heard of any letter. My curiosity was aroused. "What letter?" Linda proceeded to describe a fifteen-page, single-spaced letter with narrow margins that Richard had left on the bed the day he walked out of her life. This document had a greater resemblance to an indictment than to a letter. It summarily listed every slight or affront that Richard claimed to have experienced at the hands of Linda during their entire married life.

The first event on his list—if you can even call it an event—was after only six months of marriage. I don't remember it happening. I don't know that it even did, at least, in the way that Richard describes. But Richard never mentioned anything to me about it. Not then—not later. The first I knew of any dissatisfaction was when I saw it in the letter.

That's the way it was with most of the letter. I was familiar with some of the incidents he described. But even those that I remembered as having actually occurred were taken out of context. The events may have been accurate enough. At least, they happened. But the meaning that Richard ascribed to them was totally mistaken. It makes me angry that he didn't give me an opportunity to explain myself—to clarify what was really going on.

How in the world could Richard remember everything that he put in that letter? How could he recall back to over forty years ago?

How indeed? Linda asked a good question. I suspect that it wasn't as much a case of Richard sitting down and trying to recall all of these events. Rather, it was a case of his finally writing down what he had been carrying with him throughout their married life. Safely tucked away—out of everyone's sight but his own—Richard had harbored these slights, whether real or imagined. He may have presented a pleasant exterior, but a well-concealed resentment had been a closer companion than his wife for all those years. And this companion had helped to *push* him even further away than Linda had realized.

Richard's exterior may have treated Linda pleasantly but his interior was hostile. He demonstrated his covert hostility in the manner in which he left. His failing to say anything to Linda could be viewed as merely another attempt to avoid an uncomfortable issue. But I believe the manner in which Richard departed was more than just another in a long list of avoidant acts. It was Richard's way of "taking a shot" without having to say a word. This assumption was supported by his failure to contact Linda after leaving. The removal of just specific items from the house, being careful to keep everything else as it had been, leaving a fifteen-page indictment—these were all final touches of a pent-up bitterness.

Richard was passive, even in his aggression. His departure was finely calculated. I envisioned that it was not a scared and shaking Richard who now lived several hundred miles away. No! It was a chuckling Richard—a vindictively smirking Richard—a Richard who was reveling in the misguided thoughts of finally getting even with the woman who had hurt him so often. This vindictiveness, so artfully demonstrated in the manner of Richard's departure, is the way of bitterness.

## Conclusion

Being blocked or pushed is a consequence for a marriage characterized by conflict avoidant behavior. These two states are differentiated by several factors. One of these is time. Simple anger, being blocked, is a response to the present—some current event or action has caused displeasure. Resentment, being pushed, is a product of the past. It is always historical and represents a failure to deal with previous acts. Unresolved hurts become imbedded, harbored, and nursed. Over time, what may have begun as simple anger is classically transformed into a complex bitterness.

Another differentiating factor is the real focus of displeasure. Displeasures involve issues and people. Simple anger is more *issues* related. You may be angry with a person, but this anger is primarily because of something that was either done or not done. The issue is of significant importance. Resentment is more *person* related. When resentment is at the core of a relationship, any issue will do. It is amazing how a relatively minor issue can serve as a source of significant irritation. That is because the cited issue is not the real problem. The real problem is bitterness. The identified issue merely presents an opportunity to direct hostility toward the resented person.

A final differentiating factor is the direction of movement within the relationship. Simple anger seems to freeze positions in a relationship. A safe distance is reached and maintained. Movement toward one another is blocked, but when the anger is resolved, the mates are free to once again move toward one another and reestablish their preferred degree of closeness. Resentment is more intense. A mate desires to push the other mate away, to actively seek distance. Mates move toward each other only to attack and to express bitterness.

These differentiating factors are easily seen in the marriage of Richard and Linda. What began with incidents creating simple anger on both sides gradually grew to a complete resentment. Relational impasses, combined with history, worked to keep their relationship distant and superficial. Though Richard and Linda probably represent an extreme illustration, no couple begins as an extreme.

What happened to Richard and Linda is tragic. This is totally opposite of the design of a bonding marriage—moving toward a heightened level of intimacy and closeness. It is sad to think of any marriage ending, much less one of over forty years' duration that has brought four children to adulthood. You think of mates really being there for each other during the latter years of life. This was not to be for Richard and Linda. But what is even sadder than the ending of this relationship and of the remaining years that they will not spend together is the meager quality of relational life during the forty years they did share. What a tragic waste. Each in their own way—Linda overtly and Richard covertly—were immensely unhappy. But nothing was done to correct the problem. They just unnecessarily avoided each other until Richard was finally able to push himself right out of the marriage.

# 7

# *Self-Protection*

## Motivation #1

Dealing with any form of avoidance includes whats, hows, and whys. The whats and hows pertain to behavior. A person *is* avoidant (what) and accomplishes this goal through any one of several different *actions* (how). As behaviors, these actions are observable, identifiable, and describable. The whys pertain to motivation. They represent a conglomerate of attitudes, beliefs, and feelings. Unlike behaviors, the whys are often hidden, making accurate identification a challenging task. However, this difficulty in recognition does not lessen their importance. Quite the contrary—*the motivation for a behavior is frequently of greater significance than the behavior itself.*

It is the whys (motivations) that largely determine behavior. That is why I frequently cite the importance of knowing why you do what you do. Beliefs, emotional comfort levels, feelings, attitudes—these all work together in both causing and maintaining avoidant behavior and are the core. The key to behavioral change does not rest in realizing that you are avoidant, though this is necessary. Neither does it rest in identifying the specific manner utilized in your avoidance, although this is also important. The real key to change rests with discovering and resolving what is at the root of your behavior—

"What motivates you?" Once the attitude that exists behind the tendency to avoid is discovered, correction is possible.

As a therapist, I have observed five common themes that have long motivated husbands and wives to avoid dealing with dissatisfactions within their marriages. Each of the next five chapters will identify a common motivation for conflict avoidant behavior. As you work through these chapters, take special note of the themes that seem to most reflect the way you believe and feel. Taking your own pulse could prove to be a helpful step in improving your own relationship.

## Dallas and Melody

Dallas was dressed a little differently than most of my other clients. With his boots, hat, and vest, he appeared readier for an episode of *Gunsmoke* than he did a counseling session in urban America. But for Dallas, this was normal attire. He was involved in the country music industry and could have donned the traditional western look as a costume. But in knowing both the man and his history, there was no mistaking Dallas for any kind of rhinestone cowboy. There was nothing he enjoyed more than riding horses and herding cattle. He sang and looked the part of the music industry, but he was also a real cowboy.

The two of us sat in my office. That wasn't how the session was planned. Dallas's wife, Melody, was supposed to have come as well. But at the last moment, and in complete exasperation, she had sent Dallas on by himself. "You go. I'm not up to it. I think it's too late anyway. Just go on!"

I had only seen Dallas and Melody a few times, and our contact had been spread over several months. They had come in for one session a year earlier at Melody's insistence. She was upset and ready to quit then as well. We had scheduled a second session, but it had been canceled because Dallas had to go out of town. Things between them seemed to improve, and another appointment was never scheduled. It was now one year and another crisis later. Once again, Melody was at the end of her rope, and it was time to see a counselor.

We had met the week before to view the complaints. Even though it had been a year since our previous contact, it was as if no time had passed. The complaints, the illustrations, the intensity of emotion—all of these were the same. Nothing had changed. Melody explained the situation.

What's the use? I feel like my complaints just fall on deaf ears. I know it's hard when people try to adjust to the type of schedule we have. Dallas is gone 50 percent of the time. Just about the time we get the family routine down to account for his absence, he comes home, and we have to go through another adjustment. It's hard.

We could do this if Dallas would just work with me on it. But he won't. Anytime I try to talk to him about my frustrations—anytime I try to get him to help me work on some solutions—he just shuts me out. It's like talking to a wall. He completely shuts down on me. He won't say a word. I just get this glassy-eyed stare. "Hello. Is anybody home?" I can't live like this. I won't live like this! I refuse. I'm through!

Dallas sat motionless during Melody's indictment. He just stared. This was probably similar to what occurred between him and Melody at home. I commented on this seeming lack of connection and asked what was going on with him. Dallas shook his head and responded, "I don't know." I pressed him a little harder. "No, Dallas. That's not good enough. What's going on inside of you? What are you thinking? What are you feeling?" There was a pause. I was comfortable with the silence and willing to let a long period of time go by before rescuing Dallas. I didn't have to wait long.

It bothers me when Melody gets upset. I can't help it. I know she's not hollering and screaming or anything like that. But she might as well be. I just have a difficult time with her not being happy with me.

I guess I feel rejected. And I really don't like the feelings that come when I think she's rejecting me. I know that sounds wimpy. I can't help it. When she comes at me with these complaints, I just want to crawl in a hole and hide. Maybe that's what I do. I crawl up inside and hide until she calms down. I just find it too uncomfortable to deal with her when she's not happy with me.

"I can't live like this. I won't live like this! I refuse. I'm through!" These were Melody's words at our previous session. But these were also the words that she had spoken a year earlier. I have found that just because someone *says* they are through doesn't necessarily *mean* they are through. But things weren't looking good. Where was Melody? It was she, not Dallas, who had initiated coming back to counseling. I asked Dallas what he thought all of this meant. He was slow to respond. But when he did, his words were somber.

Melody may mean it this time. I don't know when I've seen her this tired and discouraged. She says she's heard me say "I'll do better" too many times for it to make much of a difference now. *I think Melody may have already given me my last "last chance."*

I didn't know whether the last part of Dallas's statement was a line from an actual country song or whether it was just an ideal sentiment for a new one. It ended up being prophetic. Melody had reached the end of her rope. She had given Dallas his last "last chance." She was no longer willing to wait for him to deal with her. She was through.

## Thomas and Meghan

Dallas demonstrated a rather passive form of self-protection. He was avoidant, and his motivation related to his personal discomfort with even the thought of rejection. But Dallas was not sitting on his own dissatisfactions. He was actually quite content with the marriage. The problem was that Dallas refused to deal with Melody regarding *her* dissatisfactions. Melody would approach Dallas, but out of fear he refused to deal. This avoidant response only created greater friction and ultimately resulted in a crisis in their marriage.

The variation of self-protection demonstrated by Dallas and Melody is far different from that presented by Thomas and Meghan. Again, it was the husband who chose to be avoidant. And again, the motivation was self-protection. Thomas also had a difficult time with even the thought of being rejected. But he actually played a more active part in this avoidance. Unlike Dallas, there were things in the marriage that Thomas did not like. He believed that Meghan was insensitive to his needs and to the things that he viewed as important. And he thought that at times her behavior was selfish. So from time to time, Thomas became discontent, but rather than deal directly with Meghan regarding these issues, out of fear of her reaction he just stuffed his displeasure.

Thomas's choice to be self-protectively avoidant gradually took its toll on him and his marriage. He and Meghan were part of the young, well-educated, upwardly mobile segment of American society. He was a corporate executive who looked the part by wearing conservative business suits and starched shirts and acted the part by spending long hours at the office. (I asked Thomas if he preferred to be called Tom. He quickly informed me he was a Thomas, not a Tom.)

Executive lifestyles can be hectic. Though Thomas's schedule was demanding, a relationship could be noticed between his level of displeasure with Meghan and the number of hours he spent at the office. The greater his displeasure, the less Meghan saw of him. She began to notice this ever-increasing absence. Ultimately it became a source of tension. Thomas explained:

> I dealt with Meghan by *not* dealing with her. I just stayed at the office. You can always find more things to do. That's the kind of work I'm in. You're never caught up. But that wasn't why I worked late. I was angry with Meghan and I was just too afraid to face her. So I stayed away.
>
> Meghan began to notice I was staying at the office for longer and longer hours. First she just complained about my absence. "What's taking so much of your time? How much longer will this have to go on?" Then she began to suspect there was a reason for my staying away that was other than work. She figured out I wasn't happy and asked me about it. But I continued to avoid her. Finally, she stopped caring whether I was at home or not.
>
> That's where things are now. We're both miserable, and neither of us knows what to do. We aren't even sure if we know what we

want. It's a mess. I'm still scared to tell her what I think. I just can't do it. There's no telling what she might say or do.

## Fearing a Mate's Response

Dallas and Thomas shared little in common. One enjoyed a gallop on a horse while the other relished handling a fine European automobile. One liked blue jeans, boots, and cowboy hats while the other appreciated the feel of an all-cotton, pinpoint, button-down shirt. And while one felt at home with the chaos of the entertainment world—the travel, the stage, and the fans—the other preferred the calm offered by the all-cherry interior of a fine office in an executive suite. They were little alike—Dallas and Thomas—except when it came to fears. Each could aptly state, "I fear my mate's response." And this common fear was the primary force behind the behavior they shared. Each was avoidant.

Sometimes fears are justified. If dealing with a mate regarding dissatisfactions results in excessive and abusive reactions, then avoidance may be warranted and even advisable. (This form of elected avoidance would be for the short term while the more pressing issues of safety and treatment for behavioral change were addressed.) There is a time and place for wisdom. But if fear is not the result of excess then it needs to be faced and resolved.

Neither Dallas's nor Thomas's spouse represented a real threat to their safety—there was no physical abuse or rage, though they may become upset. No! The problem of avoidance in these two marriages rested in the irrational fears of the avoiders.

## Challenging Our Fears

The irrationalness of fears of this type rests in two areas. The first area is the anticipation of the dreaded action—the assumption that the feared action will actually happen. An example would be the following statement: "If I tell Mary that it makes me angry when she discounts my feelings, she'll criticize me even more." Whether in form of overt rejection and rebuff or a more subtle disappointment, the avoider supposes that his mate's response will be negative. I call this irrational because the avoidant mate does not know for a fact that this anticipated response will occur. He only presumes. It could be that his mate's response would be positive. In spite of this, the anticipation of rejection in the mind of the avoider is the next thing to reality. The avoider lives by the motto "because I think it, it must be so."

The second area of irrational fear is catastrophizing an actual event. The spouse was rejecting, or she did rebuff her mate, or she did appear disappointed in him because of what he had to say. Catastrophizing is irrational because of the significance and meaning assigned to this response by the avoidant mate. This can be illustrated by adding to the statement cited above. "If I tell Mary that it makes me angry when she discounts my feelings, she'll criticize me even more. And that will be terrible!" Catastrophizing does not distort the reality of occurrence, only the degree of significance. The anticipated and feared reaction, when and if it occurs, *is* terrible!

We all like to be liked. We all want to be accepted. And we all dislike the alternatives. But to say that the latter is terrible just isn't reality. It may be too bad when people do not accept what we say. It may be unfortunate when there is conflict and upset between us and our mates. And it may be extremely uncomfortable. But it is not terrible. We will survive the experience, though we sometimes doubt it.

Being overly sensitive to criticism, hypersensitive to personal rejection, fearful of a mate's disappointment, or questioning whether you can stand it if your spouse becomes upset with you are examples of interpersonal excesses that are usually *brought into* a marriage as opposed to having been *developed within* the relationship. They are natural tendencies that we have developed through childhood experiences. They may be partially the result of family dynamics but could also be products of other life events such as experiences with peers. Exploring the origin of these tendencies could be helpful in bringing understanding, clarification, and eradication. However, it is not likely that the discomfort associated with these fears will disappear through insight or understanding alone, or prior to a change in your behavior. And discomfort may never completely disappear. However, fears must still be faced and behaviors changed.

I remember when I first understood the meaning of the word *bravery.* I had superficially associated it with heroic acts performed by fearless men and women. Then I realized the truer meaning— that bravery didn't really have as much to do with the lack of fear as it did with the willingness of people to courageously act in spite of their fear. Courageous action is what changes avoidant behavior motivated by the fear of a spouse's possible reaction. The fear does not totally go away. Nor does the discomfort associated with the displeasure totally disappear. We just choose to do what is right in spite of our fear and our discomfort.

It is amazing what can happen when a mate faces his fear. One mate, who had long been controlled by the fear of his wife's possible response, put it this way:

> I finally decided that I wasn't going to let fear control the rest of my life. I began to deal with Cindy instead of avoiding her. It wasn't easy at the start. It still isn't. But it's gotten better. And you know what—I found that *I didn't die!*
>
> I used to think that if she got upset with something I said or did that it would be the end of the world—that I couldn't stand it— that I'd just die. But that's not the case. She's gotten upset with me lots of times since then, and I haven't died yet. We just deal with the problem, and it gets better.

Desiring calmness and acceptance over upset and rejection is the norm. It's just not realistic to expect these all the time. And when the upsets come, as uncomfortable as they may be, we do not die. And neither do our marriages if we will just learn to deal instead of allowing fear to control our lives.

# 8

# *Overprotection*

## Motivation #2

Steve was afraid of conflict. Debbie was all too aware of this. Through eighteen years of marriage she had watched Steve stuff, deny, and rationalize away even the most minor irritations.

> I could always tell when Steve was upset about something. He would get fidgety. He's so transparent. But he would never say anything to me about it. He just acted as if everything was fine.
>
> It has always been that way. At first, it took me a little while to pick up on it. Early in the marriage, when I sensed Steve was unhappy about something, I would approach him about it. But this seemed to make him so uncomfortable that I just stopped.
>
> I really don't like to see Steve hurting. He has the same nervous reaction when I try to talk about something that I'm not happy about. He's sooo sensitive! After realizing what was going on, I gave up trying to deal with Steve about anything of a conflictual nature. It just wasn't worth all the pain he seemed to go through.

Debbie knew that Steve had come by his tendencies—being overly sensitive, fearing rejection, and avoiding conflict—honestly. His father had been extremely overbearing and difficult to approach. No matter how hard Steve had tried, he could never seem to please his dad. Steve's father believed that his high standards and special means of encouragement would ultimately make Steve a more successful person. All that his form of encouragement seemed to foster in Steve was a nervousness whenever he encountered even the possibility of rejection and a hypersensitivity to failure.

Recognizing Steve's tendencies and understanding where they came from, Debbie was committed to circumventing any unnecessary hardships for the husband she loved. Consequently, when she began to notice him becoming increasingly quiet, she concealed her concern with a smile. Her response was similar when she began to notice financial irregularities. Inside, Debbie was beginning to feel stress and anxiety. But her outward appearance continued to be cool, calm, and collected. This pleasant exterior disappeared when, after two years of intentionally avoiding an unknown *something,* Debbie discovered that Steve had not only brought them to the brink of financial ruin, but he also had created an elaborate scheme of deception to keep the knowledge from her.

Steve was not a dishonest man. But he had made some unwise financial decisions that resulted in significant losses for him and Debbie. Steve feared Debbie's reaction should she become aware of his failure. Rather than sharing this information, he devised a means of keeping it secret. He reasoned, "Debbie would be very upset with me if she knew, and I don't think I could stand that." With the passage of time, and an increasingly unwieldy labyrinth of deception, Steve's proverbial house of cards finally came crashing down around him. The disclosure of the deception brought their marriage to a crisis.

By now, you have identified Steve as self-protective. It would be tempting to lay the responsibility for the avoidance in this marriage at his feet. But that would be an error. What was Debbie's role in this marital mishap? Did she contribute to the avoidance pattern? As we scrutinize their marriage, it becomes apparent that this was not a case of either/or. This was a case of both mates being avoidant, each for a different motivation.

## Not Wanting to Hurt a Mate's Feelings

Steve was very intent on avoiding even the slightest possibility of Debbie's disapproval. But while his error was in *self*-protection, Debbie's was in *over*protection. Debbie did not want to hurt Steve. As a result, she did everything within her control to shield him from personal discomfort. Together, they cooperatively worked for the same goal—to protect Steve. As it turned out, this marriage would have been far better served had the relationship been prioritized above the comfort levels of either member.

The theme that underscores the overprotective motivation is this: "I do not want to hurt my mate's feelings." This theme was repeatedly expressed by Debbie as she attempted to shield Steve from any discomfort. Not all couples have as cooperative an arrangement as did Steve and Debbie. Steve was overly sensitive and Debbie wished to honor his needs for avoidance. In most marriages where overprotection is found, however, this form of avoidance is not requested by the mate who is being protected. Rather, it totally emanates from the varying needs of an overprotective mate—like Debbie.

One client, Cathy, found that her overprotective behavior came from a strong need to be over responsible. She had been raised in a chaotic home. There had been a series of men in her mother's life, none of whom adequately served in the role of father. And her mother, though proficient enough in bearing children, was hardly suited to caring for them. As the oldest child, Cathy took on the role of caring for her younger siblings. In part, she genuinely cared for her siblings. But her efforts were also an attempt to bring some sense of order and calm to her home life. Cathy became a "fix it" person, and this tendency to be over responsible—"I can make it better"—followed Cathy into adulthood. It was demonstrated in her marriage through her decision to not confront her husband. Cathy reasoned, "Why bother Bob when it's my responsibility to fix what is wrong anyway?"

Debbie has already demonstrated the characteristic of being *too nice*. This form of overprotection is motivated by love. Debbie loved Steve too much to hurt him, so she protected him instead. I cannot argue with Debbie's intent. Nor do I wish to discount the love that Debbie obviously felt for Steve. But when wanting to be nice interferes with healthy behavior, and when we associate loving someone with unhealthy behavior, there is at least confusion on the part of the avoider. Somewhere, being nice and loving has crossed a line of excess and represents some faulty assumptions.

Jan, another client, behaved overprotectively because of a strong tendency to feel guilty. In part, this was encouraged by her husband. Gary seemed to know just what to say. Whenever Jan attempted to deal with him regarding some dissatisfactions, he would respond with statements such as, "I thought you loved me!" and "There goes our marriage." Even though Gary exploited the guilt angle, he would not have been successful if Jan had not already been prone to feeling guilty, which was natural for her. We were uncertain of its origin. But the fact that it influenced her behavior was unquestioned. Whenever a dissatisfaction would arise, Jan would reason, "If I have a problem with what Gary is doing, it's really my problem—not his. I don't have the right to put Gary through all of this stress." The guilt produced by this line of thinking immediately stopped any of Jan's effort to deal with her dissatisfaction.

A final word on the theme, "I do not want to hurt my mate's feelings." Sometimes the claim is false. This is the case when a mate who claims to be overprotective is actually self-protective. He may report that his avoidant behavior is due to his love and caring for his wife when actually he fears her reaction. It seems that there is less stigma associated with overprotection than self-protection. In the minds of some mates, it is more socially acceptable to be too caring than it is to be fearful.

## An Issue of Intent

Rita was obviously perplexed as she sat in my office. There were several things happening in her marriage that had displeased her for quite some time. But her standard response had been avoidance. Early attempts to deal with Mike regarding her concerns had resulted in strategic maneuvers on his part. He had been visibly bothered by the pressure exerted by Rita. Being a compassionate woman, "Mike's pain became her pain," and Rita began to protect him from her true feelings.

We were now several years along the marital journey. As Rita sat in my office, she made it clear that she was tired of protecting Mike and that she desired their relationship to be different. "But I feel so guilty when I upset him. It doesn't seem right for me to hurt him that way." Not wanting to see Mike hurt was both compassionate and admirable. It reflected a right heart. But to allow this attitude to control her behavior was both excessive and irrational. Rita's confusion rested with a misperception about her intent.

"What is your intent, Rita?" I asked her. "In dealing with Mike, what are you *really* trying to do? Are you trying to hurt him? Is it your goal to be spiteful—to inflict pain? Are you resisting him, attempting to demonstrate your power and control? Are any of these your goal?" Rita sat silently for a few moments before responding. I had already met with her for several sessions. Knowing her as I did, I knew what her response would be before she even answered.

No. That's not what I'm trying to do. I just want to do what's *right*—what's healthy. I want our marriage to be better.

Rita needed to look long and hard at her intent. In reality, her dealing honestly and directly with Mike may in fact cause him some discomfort. But that is not why she does what she does. Rita's goal was to behave in a healthy way. If her doing so would prompt some discomfort, pain, frustration, or hurt for Mike, that would be unfortunate. But it would neither be terrible nor should it be avoided.

Rita was facing a boundary issue. She was confused about where her responsibility began and ended. In her relationship with Mike, Rita needed to take responsibility for and appropriately handle her behavior and her feelings. To do less would have been irresponsible. To do more, however, would have been over responsible. When Rita adapted her behavior in an attempt to prevent Mike from experiencing some emotional discomfort, she was actively extending her boundary of responsibility beyond herself to include Mike's feelings. She was not only assuming responsibility for her own feelings but for Mike's as well.

Mike was an adult. He needed to be responsible for having, acknowledging, and dealing with his feelings in an appropriate manner. Overprotection robbed him of this opportunity. In essence, Rita was preventing Mike from behaving as an adult. As Rita began to accept the concept of healthy boundaries, she was able to relinquish what was truly Mike's responsibility. She allowed him to be an adult—to experience the feelings of adulthood and to accept the responsibility that goes with the title.

Pain is part of life. Though we do not seek to inflict it needlessly, there are times when it is unavoidable. Our intent, as was Rita's, is to do what is in the best interest of the relationship even when so doing causes discomfort. We do this because we are adults and because we strive to behave in a healthy manner.

## Establishing Boundaries

The presence of overprotection indicates the absence of relational boundaries. Effectively dealing with this form of conflict avoidance requires that appropriate boundaries be established. This is not usually a comfortable task but is necessary nonetheless. The task of establishing healthy boundaries in a marriage is easier when we embrace the following principles.

### 1. Clearly recognize and define where healthy boundaries lie.

What are your personal limits? What exactly is your responsibility? What is healthy and what is not? In establishing a relational boundary, your goal is to clearly determine what you are responsible for and what you are not.

- You *are* responsible for what *you do.*
- You *are* responsible for what *you feel.*
- You *are not* responsible for either *the behavior or feelings of others.* This responsibility belongs to them. Let them have it.

### 2. Pain is part of life.

From birth to the grave, we cannot escape the reality of pain and discomfort. It is part of human existence. Though we prefer as little pain as possible, we are far better off facing our discomfort than either fleeing from it or trying to avoid its every occurrence. After all, if the truth were known, some of our greatest times of personal and relational growth have come from our encounters with pain.

### 3. Every adult deserves the right to be treated as an adult.

You treat an adult as an adult when you allow him to be responsible for himself—when you do not take personal responsibility for his behavior or feelings. To do otherwise is patronizing. In a condescending manner, you are questioning the capability of your mate. Every adult has the right to demonstrate responsibility. Do not usurp this privilege.

### 4. Mates are seldom so fragile that they cannot be treated as adults.

Your mate will not die if you deal with him. You may think he will. He may even think he will. But trust me, he won't and neither will you. When working with clients who have conflict avoidance problems, I frequently give them the opportunity to deal within the confines of a counseling session. The result is always the same and often surprising to both mates—no one dies!

Whether or not the particular issue is resolved is not as important as the new reality grasped through this experience. Previously, the mates just thought that one of them was too fragile to handle confrontation. Now by witnessing their own survival and their mate's, they realize this is not the case, and the myth of fragility is dispelled.

### 5. Know your intent.

Be certain of your motives. Certainly what you have to say may create some hurt, disappointment, or frustration. But is this your primary aim or are these merely by-products of a more noble goal? What is your intent? If your intent is to inflict pain, your motives need to be addressed. If your intent is to behave in an emotionally honest manner and to allow your mate the opportunity to do likewise, you are allowing an adult to be an adult, which is far more important than any emotional discomfort that may inadvertently occur.

# 9

# *Rationalization*

## Motivation #3

Becky demonstrated as much intensity as I had ever seen in my office. She had not always been this way. But marriage sometimes brings out the worst in people. She and her husband, Todd, had been separated for over three months, and we were just now beginning to talk about the possibility of reconciling their relationship. At least, we were talking about their talking. A great deal of hostility was present in this relationship, and Todd and Becky were not even to the point of sitting together in the same room to discuss the possibility of reuniting. I was having to meet with each of them separately. It was obvious that there would have to be some resolution of the hostility that engulfed both partners before either one would consider a move from the safety of separateness to the risk of togetherness.

I couldn't help but wonder what had happened. I doubted that their marriage had begun with this level of intensity. What had occurred to create such animosity between them? Had there been an incident of some kind—some isolated injury that had resulted in deeply harbored resentment? Or had the problem been a pattern wound—something that would have had little if any effect had it occurred only once, but due to repetition grew increasingly more painful as a pattern of frequency emerged?

All of my inquiries suggested that this marriage of ten years had begun as peacefully and optimistically as most. Todd and Becky each willingly said "I do." Each had dreams of what their life together would bring. Each had expectations of what they would invest and of what they desired from the other. It was apparent that somewhere along their journey, things had begun to change. And when they did, hostility began to develop.

For Becky and Todd, trouble developed around what each brought into the marriage, the way trouble emerges for many marriages. Becky expected a great deal from marriage—probably too much. She had high aspirations for status, which involved Todd's career achievement and economic success. When these status needs were not readily met, Becky sensed dissatisfaction. Todd needed to deal with Becky about her expectations so that adjustments could be made, but he did not. Todd also had desires and expectations, but none more pressing than peace. You can guess his response to Becky's excesses—avoidance!

From the very beginning of their marriage, Becky dealt with her dissatisfactions, even though they may have been inappropriate, by approaching Todd. She was frustrated and wanted him to deal with her. Todd refused. He ignored her admonitions, he pretended to not hear her comments, and he even began to stay away from home. These maneuvers only heightened Becky's frustration. She described Todd's behavior as insensitive and interpreted his motivation as a lack of genuine caring and concern.

> At first, I would approach Todd about my dissatisfactions. I tried everything. I was nice—then I was not so nice. I waited for just the right time only to find that there was no right time. I even tried writing him letters. This too failed. Todd just wasn't interested in what I had to say. (Her interpretation of his avoidance.)
>
> Finally, I gave up. What was the use in trying? It wasn't going to make any difference. He wasn't going to change. My pressing him wasn't going to get anything resolved. It wasn't going to get me what I wanted. So why keep it up? I got tired of beating my head

against a wall and quit trying altogether. When I had a problem, I just started keeping it to myself.

I thought I could handle my frustration that way. I told myself, "Just ignore it and it will go away." But that's not what happened. I got mad. And then I got madder.

Becky started out dealing with her dissatisfactions. Then she rationalized, "What's the use? It isn't going to change anything." So she stopped. Now she was bitter, and their marriage was on the brink of dissolution.

## A Repetitive History

Rationalization as a motivation for avoidance is supported by a strong belief that nothing can be done to change what is happening. This theme is followed by what appears very logical—if nothing is going to make any difference, why not quit doing everything and just let things go on as they are? There seems to be no point in wasting time and energy on futility.

As with the other motivations for avoidance, rationalization has some distinguishing characteristics. One is a history of repetitive attempts to deal with dissatisfaction, all of which have met with failure. Mates who rationalize base their belief on repetitive experience, not just the result of one unsuccessful attempt.

Repetitiveness was evident in Becky's account of her marriage to Todd. "At first, I would approach Todd about my dissatisfactions. I tried everything.... Finally, I gave up." The theme of "I used to do better" is also often expressed whenever I speak with rationalizing mates. Though varied avenues may have been tried by these mates in attempting to deal with their reluctant spouses, each admits that there was a time when they did a better job. Years of effort with no apparent change finally took their toll. It was the previously non-avoidant spouses who ultimately decided to change from dealing to avoiding.

The pattern is clear. They "grew weary of well doing." With the weariness came exasperation. Ultimately, they resigned to what appeared to be the inevitable. "I've tried to deal, but he just continues to avoid me. Things will never be any different. I might as well give up." Weary and frustrated, this is exactly what they do, if not completely, at least in part. In a moment of reflection, one over-whelmed wife remarked, "I didn't give up altogether. But I just found my attempts to be less and less frequent." For her marriage, it was almost the same as quitting because it achieved the same result.

## Justification

The rationalizer's theme of "what's the use" was demonstrated by Becky. She had tried and tried to get Todd to deal with her—all to no avail. Finally, she gave up. What is interesting about Becky's account of her marital history is that there was an air of legitimacy associated with her decision to give up. This nonproductive, avoidant stance seemed perfectly acceptable to her. Was this air of accept-ability unique to the marriage of Becky and Todd? Or was this ten-dency to feel almost justified in doing nothing more widespread?

There was nothing exceptional about Becky's attitude. Feeling justified in doing nothing is another characteristic of those who choose to rationalize their avoidant behavior. After all, they have already tried and tried to inaugurate dealing into the marriage.

Believing that it won't make any difference results in an attitude of justification for doing nothing. Once entrenched, this attitude makes changing behavior a difficult task. Avoidance has been legit-imized, and why should anyone stop doing something that is clearly legitimate? Another client, Randy, illustrates just how powerful this attitude of justification can be.

> For years I felt justified in avoiding dissatisfactions. This was true whether they were either complaints that I might have or something that was bothering Judy. I mean, what was the use? Judy said she wanted me to deal with her, but that really wasn't the case. The first time she heard something that she didn't like, she'd just get upset.
>
> Why fight it? I mean, nothing was going to change. I learned that the hard way. It just became evident that I was going to be far bet-ter off—in fact, we were both going to be better off—if I just didn't bother with anything. I really was doing our marriage a service. If nothing was going to change, I might as well keep peace instead of creating needless tension.

Randy felt justified in his avoidance. His rationalization that nothing would change in his attempts to deal with Judy convinced him that everyone would be better off, and would remain calmer, if he was avoidant. He was even proud of his behavior. After all, his actions were for the ultimate good of all concerned.

## "It's a Lie!"

I was conducting a seminar on avoidance. When we came to rationalization as a motivation for avoiding conflict, I asked the question, "What is wrong with this reason for avoidance?" Spontaneously, and so quickly that it startled the other seminar participants, one husband shouted out, "It's a lie!" Gary had not calculated his response. Had he thought about it, he may have said nothing or at least would have been calmer in his observation. But his response was purely impulsive—and purely honest.

With the exception of a few snickers, the room grew painfully quiet. Gary was obviously embarrassed by his outburst. I don't know whether his next words were motivated by an overwhelming need to defend himself or whether he just reasoned that since he was already in the water, he might as well swim. Either way, having captured everyone's attention, Gary began to elaborate.

When I'm rationalizing, I'm telling myself: "It won't make any difference." That's a lie. Believe me, I know! I've tried it and lived it. There is nothing further from the truth. Being avoidant always makes a difference.

I used to keep from telling Cheryl things all the time. It didn't matter how significant or insignificant, I just told myself that it wouldn't make any difference. "She won't ever find out"; "She would only get upset if she knew"; "It wouldn't change anything anyway." I rationalized everything. I found all of these to be false.

Doing nothing *does* something—it always does. You cannot avoid things in your marriage without there being some consequence. It took my marriage coming to a crisis three years ago for me to realize that. Now, I always deal. No matter how small, I deal with Cheryl. Things are much better but I'm still paying the price. There are times when Cheryl still asks me if I'm telling her the whole truth—

if I'm telling her everything. It's hard to get trust back after you've blown it the way I did. But step-by-step, we're getting there.

In the purest sense, Gary's critique was against the theme "it won't make any difference." Gary wasn't as interested in whether dealing with a mate would bring any change in his or her behavior as he was in the impact that avoidant behavior would ultimately have on the relationship. This is why his observation "doing nothing *does* something" is so profound. Avoidance always has a consequence. A further evaluation of Gary's self-disclosure shows that he was not only rationalizing, he was also being self-protective. It's not unusual to find avoidant behavior supported by a combination of motivations.

Rationalization is another case of having faulty boundaries—being confused about where our responsibilities lie and where they do not. This issue of boundaries is key to both individual and marital health. Over the past several months, I have been developing a manuscript around the theme that health is contagious. Though healthy individuals do not *control* the actions of others (nor do we aspire to), we do *influence* their behavior. Being persistent in doing good (see Gal. 6:9) can have a significant impact on those around us—including our spouse. This is a concept that is sadly neglected by rationalizers.

For healthy boundaries to be established in a relationship, four elements must be blended together.

### 1. Recognize your level of responsibility.

You are responsible for your behavior—no more and no less. Boundaries determine where your responsibility begins and where it ends.

You cannot make a mate deal with dissatisfactions, whether they are yours or his. Choosing to behave in a healthy manner is a decision for which he must be responsible. But you are responsible for your own behavior regardless of his choices. Draw your boundary! Recognize and assume responsibility for what you are responsible for—your own behavior. You are not responsible for the outcome, only for doing what is right.

### 2. Be certain of your primary goal.

Sometimes we confuse the goals of our actions. It's not that we do not desire to positively influence the behavior of those around us. We do. But if our focus is more on influence than on personal responsibility, it is easy for our actions to become manipulative and our frustrations to increase if the desired change does not occur.

A healthy focus is one that emphasizes doing what is right above outcome. Change in a mate is then a secondary goal and an added bonus. Regardless of any change in the behavior of a mate, you have a level of personal satisfaction that comes with knowing you have behaved in a healthy way.

### 3. Choose to behave in a healthy way.

Healthy behavior is not always natural and automatic. If it were, more people would do it. But whether behavior is good, bad, or somewhere in between, it is always the result of choice.

There are many reasons why we sometimes behave inappropriately. Frequently the reason has to do with comfort levels. It is sometimes emotionally uncomfortable to do the right thing. When this is the case, you are forced to choose between comfort and discomfort. Are you going to continue nonproductive behavior, even though it may be the most comfortable choice, or are you going to behave in a healthy way? The choice is yours.

### 4. Maintain an attitude of health.

Though behavioral change is not the primary goal, it is still a desired result. If health is contagious, and I believe it is, behaving in a healthy manner is the best influence for change in those with whom we interact.

Remember *why* you do *what* you do. Maintaining an attitude of health will help you establish a level of responsible behavior.

The four elements just described work together to establish healthy boundaries in marriage. They also categorically challenge the tendency to rationalize. "It won't make a difference" *is* a lie. It is only by maintaining healthy behavior—continuing to deal and continuing to state needs—that change can happen. "So let us never tire of doing good, for if we do not slacken our efforts we shall in due time reap our harvest" (Gal. 6:9).

# 10

# Misbelief

## Motivation #4

Michael was a quiet man. When considering his countenance, his manner of interacting with people, and his accomplishments in life, probably no term was more accurate than "unassuming." It was Michael's unassuming nature that ultimately caused his wife, Stacy, to seek counseling—and she brought Michael with her.

There are several adages that attempt to describe what actually takes place in the mate selection process. One of these is "birds of a feather flock together"—the attraction of people to those with similar personalities, interests, socioeconomic status, and values. Another is "opposites attract"—the reverse of the first adage, suggesting that differences and not similarities seem to attract. We all know marriages that seemingly prove each of these two categories. There is another saying that seems to go hand-in-hand with this latter adage—not only do opposites *attract,* they also *attack.* The characteristics that may have been previously admired soon become despised. And when this is the case, dissatisfaction arises.

Michael and Stacy were opposites. Michael was quiet and unassuming, which made him easy to be around—that is, if your expectations were for minimal interaction, minimal initiative, and minimal follow-through. He seemed to have a great tolerance for chaos, whether in his personal life or anywhere he happened to be. Church, work, home—it made little difference to Michael; he just went with the flow. Stacy's perspective of Michael's nature had changed over the course of their marriage. She had moved from viewing him as easygoing to irresponsible. With the change in perspective had come frustration.

Stacy despised chaos. She needed order. Stacy was not obsessive or pathological in her needs. She just believed that life ought to function with some sort of regularity. Houses needed to be relatively free of clutter. Lawns needed to be mowed, at least occasionally. Bills needed to be paid on time. If you said you would do something then you should do it. Stacy could tolerate a normal degree of disorder, but when life became chaotic—and it seemed that living with Michael fostered chaos—she became increasingly uncomfortable.

Michael did not mind the chaos. He just allowed it to happen. This comfort was in part due to what he had learned over the years—when things get chaotic enough, someone, other than himself, will step in and take care of things. Stacy was just such a someone. She could not stand to allow things to get too out of hand. Consequently, she was always stepping in and cleaning up after Michael, whether it was the clutter he left around the house or other more significant responsibilities that he just failed to fulfill.

From the perspective of marital dynamics, Michael and Stacy had what can be described as an over/under functioner relationship. Michael was under functioning, not pulling his fair share of the load. Stacy, on the other hand, was over functioning, doing too much. Stacy did not like the dynamic, and she definitely did not want things to continue as they were. But she saw no other acceptable choice. Stacy far preferred her role of pitching in and doing things herself than the alternative of just allowing them to go undone.

When chaos finally gave way to counseling, Michael and Stacy had been married for ten years. These had not been easy years. The couple had begun their family early on; this made it difficult for Stacy to fit into the job market. She would have been content to stay at home with their two children, but Michael's employment was always unstable. He was frequently laid off. This kept them financially pressed. But it was not finances that created Stacy's dissatisfaction. It was Michael's way of dealing with life in general—and with her in particular—that created her frustration.

Stacy was frustrated with life. But more significantly, she was frustrated with Michael. As we spent some time talking about her complaints, Stacy finally made a statement that poignantly summarized all of her frustrations. In it was the core of her assessment of her situation, her feelings and attitude toward Michael, and the reason why she was in my office at all—"I'll raise two children, but I refuse to raise three!" The third child, of course, being Michael.

> I can't count on Michael to do anything! Even the things he attempts to do are never completed. There are half-done projects all over the house. It doesn't make any difference how big or small, how important or unimportant. They're all the same to Michael. He just doesn't follow through on anything.
>
> He's laid off again from work. This is the fourth time in as many years. What's he going to do? If he does as he has in the past, he won't do anything. He'll just draw his unemployment. When that runs out (and not before), he'll begin to look for something else. Until then, he'll just sit around the house hoping to be called back to his job.
>
> I can't live like this. It's not his being laid off that frustrates me so. That's a part of life. But it's what Michael does when this happens—or what he *doesn't do*—that really gets to me. And that's the way he is with life. He won't deal with anything. And he won't deal with me! We can't talk about anything because he won't discuss anything with me. When I want to talk, he just sits there and stares. I don't know what's going on in his head. It's like I'm talking to a dummy. Finally, I just get up and walk away.
>
> Well, I'm tired. I'm tired of living like this. I'm tired of picking up after a grown man. I'm tired of finishing things he begins but doesn't complete. I'm tired of carrying the load that a husband— a partner in marriage—ought to carry. And I'm tired of talking to a blank wall. Something has to change. I've had it.

Michael agreed to meet with me individually, which provided an opportunity to explore his developmental history. I was interested in gaining a feel for what contributed to his present behavior. What were the events of his life? Usually we come by our behavioral patterns honestly. As we explored these events, a couple of themes began to emerge.

Michael was raised in a family with a dominant mother and a passive father. From a parenting perspective, his mother could be described as overinvolved in the lives of all of her children, not just Michael. But there were things peculiar to Michael's life that increased his mother's attention to him. He had been seriously ill in childhood. Ill enough that he was supposed to have died, but he survived. The illness left him frail, and he always seemed just a little weaker and smaller than his peers. Overprotected, pampered—these terms describe what took place following Michael's illness. His mother almost became obsessed with caring for his every need—an obsession that did not cease when Michael reached adulthood. Nor did it end with his marriage to Stacy.

Family researchers have long been aware that the motivations for parental overprotection and pampering can be varied. Sometimes the motivation is more a parent's need than any perceived need of the child. This is the case when a marriage is dissatisfying and a parent, needing an alternative source in which to invest, becomes overinvolved in the life of a child. Another example of parental need as a motivator would be the case of a parent with some personal insecurities. These insecurities make it difficult for the parent to maintain a healthy distance in the parent-child relationship.

But overinvolvement is not limited to parents either with flaws in their marriages or individual insecurities. Even healthy parents in healthy marriages can be tempted to become overinvolved in the life of a child. This is usually the case when a child is viewed as special. Overprotecting a child who has experienced a significant hardship of some kind can be seen as an appropriate response of love. Regardless of the motivation for this protective behavior, there is no question about the outcome. Parental smothering and excessive attention can have far-reaching impact on the development of a child's personality, including restricting the development of independence and autonomy in the child. That appeared to be the case with Michael.

Michael was used to being taken care of; it was comfortable. His mother had always picked up his clothes, cleaned his room, and saw to it that he had no household chores. She was always explaining to Michael's teachers why he couldn't get all of his work done like the other children. He was special. And when it came time to look for a job, who do you think made the phone calls and filled out all the applications? Right. Mother.

As a result of his history, not only did Michael like being taken care of, he grew to expect it. When Stacy came into his life, he simply replaced his mother with someone else who was supposed to fulfill the same role. It would be trite to say that Michael married his mother, but that is at least what he attempted to do. He wanted someone else to continue the job that she had started, to take care of him.

Michael's behavioral tendencies were beginning to make sense. He had come by them honestly. But what about Stacy's complaint concerning Michael's unwillingness to deal with her regarding any dissatisfactions? Where did this come from? I asked Michael if he could verify whether this was true and if it was, to give me some insight as to why he wouldn't deal with Stacy. Here was Michael's response.

> Stacy's correct. I don't talk to her when she's upset. And I don't intend to. I was raised in a good Christian home and never saw my parents argue. There was not even as much as a cross word ever spoken between them.
>
> I will always remember the advice given to me by my father: "Son, there is nothing worth getting into a fuss over." I've always tried to live with that as my guide. I just don't think it's right to deal with dissatisfactions.

Michael was clearly conflict avoidant. Though there were several motivations working together to support this behavior, the one that he described to me on this occasion is called "misbelief." Michael mistakenly believed that he was behaving properly. To do otherwise—to deal with Stacy—would be improper. Much like the other behaviors that were causing him so much difficulty, this, too, he had learned at home.

## The Only Christian Thing to Do?

Michael's decision to avoid dealing with Stacy's dissatisfactions was based on his belief that avoidance was the Christian thing to do.

In the questionnaire that I developed to measure avoidance in marriage, I tapped the presence of the motivation with this question: "For the Christian, keeping peace is more important than dealing with conflicts." Husbands and wives who shared this belief agreed with this statement. Those who did not disagreed with it. Michael would have undoubtedly been counted among the believers.

I classify this statement as a misbelief because I do not believe it is suggested by Scripture. Granted, we are to live at peace with all people (see Rom. 12:18). And we know that peacemakers are blessed (see Matt. 5:9). But nowhere in Scripture is it suggested that peacemakers avoid dealing with dissatisfactions. In many instances, dealing is the only way peace may come. As was instructed by Jesus, when we have a problem with "a brother," we are to "go and make your peace" (see Matt. 5:23–24). In order to do this, we will have to deal with him.

Some of our confusion comes from misperceptions regarding anger, the belief that real Christians do not become angry. If they do, it is an indication of sin in their life. But again, Scripture does not support this belief. What Scripture does suggest is that we are to be angry and not sin (see Eph. 4:26). And we are to deal quickly and appropriately with our anger (see Matt. 5:22 and Eph. 4:26) so that it does not lead from anger to resentment. In short, the problem is not with our becoming angry but with how we resolve it.

There is nothing sinful about being angry or about being dissatisfied. But anger and dissatisfaction may lead to sin if not resolved appropriately. That is why both need to be faced rather than avoided. We are to seek peace through dealing. We are all far better off when, instead of operating under the mistaken belief that Christians should seek peace at any cost, we seek to be emotionally honest. A healthy rule of thumb would be this: "If it's significant enough to get upset about, it's significant enough to face and deal with," seems to be the best course for anyone who desires to be what Scripture supports—a true peacemaker.

## Another Case of Justification

Much like the problem of rationalization, an attitude of justification is also associated with misbelief. This can be noted in Michael's response to my question. He admitted that Stacy's assessment of him was correct, but he added that he had no intention of making any changes in his behavior. Michael's voice then did something that I had not heard before. It got strong. He was firm on this point. Was it fear that bolstered Michael? Was it concern for what Stacy might say or do if he dared deal with her? Not at all. Michael was bolstered by pride. He had no intention of changing, and he took pride in his position because he was "in the right." On this he would take his stand.

Poor Michael. He had taken very few stands in his life. And now, when he was deciding to do so, it was on faulty ground. He continued to be avoidant, and he did so with pride. After all, he was justified. It was the only Christian thing to do.

# 11

## *Denial*

## Motivation #5

Philip and Alice represent one of the more unusual cases I have counseled. This determination is based on their history, their personal idiosyncrasies, and their specific request. Philip and Alice were seeking premarital counseling. That in and of itself is not an unusual request. Many couples seek counseling prior to marriage in an attempt either to deal with issues that are already evident in the relationship or to avoid any surprises that may arise after they say "I do." What made their request a little unusual was that it came on the heels of their divorce—not from other mates but from each other. Philip and Alice were trying to determine whether they should reenter a union that three months earlier had been deemed irreconcilable.

Philip and Alice had met at work. Each had been previously married. Philip reported that his first wife had outgrown him. She was involved in a career that developed her level of social sophistication. She grew to a point where she and Philip no longer fit. It was at that point that she asked for and received a divorce. "I couldn't see trying to hold on to something that was dead. As much as it hurt, I had to let it go." Though Philip dated several women during the years that followed his divorce, he had not thought of remarriage until Alice entered his life.

Alice's previous marital history had been quite different from Philip's. Where calmness, order, and complacency seemed to characterize Philip's first marriage, Alice's was characterized by chaos, disorder, and conflict. Alice's husband had been abusive, both emotionally and physically. For twenty years, she had tolerated oppression and violence. Finally, she was able to gather together enough strength to end what had been a devastating existence. Alice had not been divorced as long as Philip. Nor had she dated as extensively. But she had been active enough socially to know what she did and did not want in a relationship. Like Philip, it was not until they dated that she felt herself ready to reenter marriage.

As Philip and Alice described their early courtship, they only used the best of terms. They were a natural. Relating was easy. There was never any discord between them. Not even a cross word. Both were attentive and sensitive to the other's needs. There was no hint of selfishness. It was as if they could read each other's minds. Cordial, comfortable, giving—each wondered: "How can it be so good?" They then decided to marry. Their description continued much in the same vein: Marriage was wonderful too! It was like living in paradise. There were no problems at all. "Things were great," said Philip. "At least, they were great until Alice asked me for a divorce."

The mood in the office became more somber with this last statement. A sternness seemed to come over Philip, and Alice became nervous. As the discussion continued, Philip developed a picture of the divorce coming as a complete surprise. There had been no hint of trouble. This suddenness seemed to bother him as much as the divorce did. It was the impulsiveness of this act—how quickly the marriage had ended—and the possibility of a repeat of Alice's impulsiveness that stymied any discussion of remarriage.

> We were married for one and a half years. It was great up until the day she asked me for a divorce. If a marriage can end when it's going that good, what's to stop this from happening again? What's to say that, if we did get remarried, Alice wouldn't hit me with another "out of the blue" experience?

I have to know why this happened. And I have to know that it won't happen again. I can't go through this again.

Philip was gun-shy. In this apprehensive state, he was looking for answers to the whys of Alice's impulsive act. He couldn't understand what had happened to their marriage, but he had a theory. Coming to counseling was actually an attempt to confirm an assessment that he had held since the divorce—"I think Alice is manic-depressive." (Philip was referring to a mental disturbance more accurately known as a bipolar disorder. The characteristics include both depressive and manic actions, depending on where the individual happens to be in his or her cycle of behavior. These behaviors are not a reaction to [caused by] external events but are the result of a chemical imbalance. Treatment involves taking a medication that replaces the absent chemical in the body, resulting in moderated behavior.)

I couldn't blame Philip for needing some answers. The events did not make sense to me either. No one leaves a truly happy marriage on a whim. Even though I was still unsure of what the answers might be, I was fairly certain of what they would *not* be. I did not think Alice had the type of mental disorder that Philip was suggesting; neither Alice's countenance nor her personal history suggested a problem of this nature. We needed more facts. And Alice seemed to be the logical one to provide us with the needed data.

There was a part of Alice that longed for Philip's assessment to be true. Alice desperately wanted to remarry Philip. A simple chemical imbalance would have been a clean and concise solution all the way around. Philip would have his rationale—chemical imbalance—and Alice would have her corrective mechanism—medication. Both Alice and Philip would feel fairly confident that there would not be a recurrence of the impulsive actions that brought their first marriage to an end. Marriage could be reentered and paradise regained.

However, I suspected that this solution was fraught with flaws, such as using the term *paradise* to describe their marriage. As much as Philip's solution may have simplified Alice's life, I further suspected that even she realized it was not the truthful answer.

## *What Is the Truth?*

Alice readied herself to respond both to Philip's description of an unsuspecting demise of a wonderful relationship and his assessment of mental instability. Would her remarks provide clarity or only heighten the confusion? What was the truth and would we now hear it?

> Even though I've had a lot of time to think things over during the last few months, I still don't know what to say. Maybe there is some truth to Philip's belief about me having a mental problem. I don't know.
>
> I thought we had a good marriage. Looking back, I have begun to realize that maybe there were some things that weren't as great as they could have been. But for the most part, the marriage was good.
>
> Philip grew increasingly irritable during the last two months of our marriage. Looking back, I think it may have been due to allergies and some medicine he was taking. But at the time, the only thing I could imagine was that he was unhappy living with me. (Philip and Alice never talked about these perceptions. Alice relied totally on assumptions.)
>
> I loved Philip. The last thing I wanted was to cause him any unhappiness. I figured that if I was creating a problem for him, I needed to get out of his life. Asking for a divorce was an act of love on my part. I wanted to protect him from any unhappiness. To my surprise, he took me up on my offer.

Well, here was a story. But was I any closer to the truth? Was Alice's impulsive act an act of love—an attempt to protect Philip? Was it impulsive at all? Already, some cracks were beginning to show in the picture of a marriage made in heaven. Alice had stated that, in reflecting on her marriage, there were some things that "weren't as great as they could have been." Maybe there was more to this situation than could be explained by either impulsiveness or overprotection. I suggested we meet for individual sessions to further explore their concerns.

It was a much more relaxed Alice who came to our next session. Meeting without Philip seemed to have at least a calming effect.

Whether it would lead to clarity remained to be seen. I began by probing the cracks in paradise to which Alice had alluded. She was hesitant. But with persistence, a truer picture of their relationship began to emerge.

Philip and Alice had both brought assets into the marriage and each had an income through employment. Alice had assumed they would pool their resources. After all, they were married. Philip preferred separateness—separate belongings, separate bank accounts, and separate bills. Alice told herself that it didn't really matter, and they did as Philip preferred. Philip sold his house and placed his money in a personal account, and they lived in Alice's house.

Philip suggested that they equally divide the monthly living expenses so each could pay his/her fair share. Alice felt that because Philip earned a larger salary and they were living in her house, his being responsible for a larger percentage of the monthly expenses would be more equitable. But Philip saw this as unfair; he believed that expenses needed to be shared equally. Alice again told herself that it didn't really matter, and they did as Philip preferred. This meant that Alice had very little discretionary money at the end of each month, but Philip was quite comfortable.

Sometimes things that *don't* really matter *do* really matter. Though there were several other instances of Philip's getting what he preferred and Alice's convincing herself that it didn't really matter, it was the difference in opinion regarding money that ultimately caused Alice's impulsive act. Philip's behaving irritably was true enough. And his irritability probably was related to his allergies and the various medications he was taking. But something else occurred to bring Alice's growing dissatisfaction to the surface.

Philip required Alice to pay for her own insurance. After all, this was her responsibility. An annual premium came due. Alice did not have the money to pay the premium and asked Philip to pay for it—something he could easily have done. He refused and suggested she get a loan from the bank. Alice told herself that it didn't really matter, got a loan, and began making payments. But something was different. With each payment, Alice sensed a heightened feeling of resentment. She wasn't sure why it bothered her so. After all, she had a good marriage; she knew that she loved Philip and that Philip loved her. What was there for her to be angry about? In spite of these good things, she was finding it harder and harder to contain her anger. Finally, she exploded.

> I don't remember much about what happened that day. I only know I got real upset. I was so angry.
>    I didn't really want a divorce. I was just mad. But Philip said okay. So what was I to do?

Alice's second explanation of their marriage was different from the first. At last, we had reached the truth. There had been trouble in paradise. Alice's response to Philip had not been unpremeditated and had not been the unprovoked reaction of a chemically imbalanced individual. It had been the emotional explosion of a human pressure cooker. Alice's way of dealing with Philip's selfishness—telling herself that it didn't really matter—had finally stopped working. She could no longer deny the truth, and when she came face to face with it, she reacted.

## Fooling Yourself and Fooling Others

Alice had been in denial. She had told herself that everything was okay. But it wasn't. She had focused on the good things in her marriage and completely overlooked the bad. Alice wasn't totally aware of what she was doing. But awareness or the lack of it does not change the facts. Denial creates a distorted reality. When you live in denial, the truth gets lost. The truth had been lost for Alice, and its emergence brought complications to her falsely construed idyllic marriage.

> I kept saying it was okay and that it didn't really matter. I guess I wanted so much for things to be right. I was blinded by this need. At least, now I can admit that things weren't perfect—that there were some things that did really matter.

Being out of the situation and taking time to reflect on the marriage had enabled Alice to gain a more realistic perspective of her relationship with Philip. But she was still operating in denial. Her particular state of denial had changed, but she was still in the country.

Alice had begun in total denial. Her strong need and desire for their relationship to be problem free prevented her from recognizing and accepting the truth. So Alice began by *fooling herself.* She totally denied that Philip's behavior bothered her, even though it really did. She summarily discounted any potential problem by telling herself that it didn't really matter. From this initial position of complete denial, Alice had progressed to admitting to herself that things were not all grand—that she and Philip had not been living in paradise. But she was still not ready to share this enlightenment with Philip. She had given up fooling herself but had progressed to *fooling others.*

Whether an effort to fool self or to fool others, denial is an unusually damaging form of avoidance. It strikes at the core of relational health. Without truth and honesty, there is no health. One of the questions used in my questionnaire to assess whether denial may exist in a marriage is this: "My mate *never* makes me angry." Mates who strongly agree with this statement are usually operating with some degree of denial in their marriage—whether in an attempt to fool themselves or to fool others.

The operative word here is *never.* As teachers and professors have been saying for years, "never say never." There are few if any absolutes in this world, and experiencing a problem-free marriage is definitely not one of them. Frustration, hurt, and disappointment are inevitable in every marriage. Hopefully, the number of incidents will not be large. But anger is a natural part of any relationship.

Alice had been unhappy in her marriage. But this was a fact that she had kept from herself. The consequence of this form of denial resulted in chaos for both her and Philip. Alice had traded one form of denial for another. Now she was fooling others. Unless she was prepared to deal with this form of denial, I could only predict that crisis would once again overtake this relationship. Whenever the truth gets lost, crisis is not far behind.

## *Is There Trouble in Paradise?*

Before asking whether some degree of denial exists in your own relationship, it is good to embrace the reality that, at least maritally speaking, "there is no paradise." Family researchers have found that if you observe couples long enough, all will display dysfunctional behavior. What seems to distinguish healthy couples from the unhealthy is the frequency in which these inappropriate behaviors occur. Healthy couples just behave dysfunctionally less often than do their unhealthy counterparts.

The secret is out. There are no perfect people—and no perfect marriages. So as I suggest how you can take the pulse of your own level of denial, rest assured that you are in good company. No one—not even you—is perfect.

### 1. Check your heart: How are you really feeling?

Assess your true feelings. The following list contains feelings common to all relationships. But how frequently do they occur in your marriage? Are these only occasional companions or are they frequent and even pervasive? The answers to these questions may indicate something very significant about your marriage even if what you are telling yourself is altogether different. How often do you feel:

- dissatisfied
- distant or lonely
- resentful
- frustrated
- hurt
- bored
- ignored
- rejected
- discounted
- confused

### 2. Be observant of behaviors: What's going on and what isn't?

Relating, giving, investing—each of these has a special meaning when it comes to marriage. Furthermore, each is a behavioral term. These aspects of a marriage are observable and measurable. Though it may be more difficult to ascertain the motivation or reason behind a behavior, at least observing what is or is not going on can give some indication of the quality of a relationship. Three areas of concern are these:

- **Are there indications of obvious inappropriateness?** There are some behaviors that are clear indications of danger regardless of what you may tell yourself. Physical abuse is a good example. No matter how much you deny that anything is wrong in your marriage, the presence of physical abuse categorically stands in the face of this denial. It is clearly wrong.

  There are many types of behavior other than physical abuse that have no place in healthy relationships. Take a look at your marriage. Is there anything going on that ought not to be occurring? If so, you need a more honest and realistic assessment of your relationship.

- **Is there a lack of constructive behavior?** Whereas the previous suggestion focused on what is occurring but should not, this suggestion looks at what is not occurring but should. What ought to be occurring if a marriage is to grow in a healthy direction?

  We tend to look for several degrees of investment. On a functional level, are mates cooperating regarding the day-to-day handling of life? Or does selfishness prevail? Is there time spent together purely for the enhancement of the marriage or are only separate activities pursued? On a deeper level, is there contact between the mates other than that of a merely superficial nature? For example, do you talk only about the children, the weather, and the mundane events of the day, or do you really share what's going on inside of you—your personal thoughts and feelings? These are some of the things to assess when looking at investment. Are any of these being omitted from your relationship?

- **Is your body trying to tell you something?** We have all seen individuals who say sweet things yet communicate an entirely different message through body language. An example is the wife who says, "No, I'm not angry with you" while gritting her teeth, clenching her fists, or having a tightly locked jaw and mouth. Obviously, this mate is in some stage of denial. There is an inconsistency between what is said and what is physi-

cally portrayed. But are there other ways this discrepancy can
be displayed?

Sometimes our physiological self tries to tell us things that
our emotional self refuses to hear. Are there times when you
have stomach trouble? Are there times when you have
headaches? Are there times when you feel exceptionally
stressed or nervous? There can be plausible reasons other than
denial for each of these physiological responses. But it would
be in your best interest to pay attention to what your body may
be trying to tell you. Is there a pattern to your physiological
symptoms? Be observant. Make sure you are aware of the
whole truth.

### 3. Facing denial: What are you going to do?

Denial presents two dilemmas. The first is when you are fooling
yourself. When you have been living in denial and are confronted
with the facts, you are forced to make a choice. You must either recognize and accept the truth or continue in denial.

The second dilemma is when you are fooling others. You are
already aware of the facts. Now your choice is not accepting the truth,
but rather what you are going to do now that you know what the truth
is. Are you going to deal with the truth or are you going to avoid it?

Neither of these dilemmas is easy to resolve. Any decision may
involve its own kind of pain. But though there may be no easy answer,
there are healthy choices. Healthy people recognize the truth instead
of operating in denial, and healthy people deal instead of avoiding.
There are no healthier choices.

# Identifying Your Motivation to Be Avoidant

Dealing with conflict avoidance involves whats, hows, and whys. The whys are our motivations, which can be quite different for couples and even for the mates in a particular marriage. In chapters 7–11, the themes that undergird the common reasons for failure to deal with dissatisfactions were identified. For the purpose of this exercise, each theme is in the form of a statement. As you evaluate your own avoidant behavior, ask which of these lie at the core of your decision. Two scales are provided, offering an opportunity for both partners to respond. Place a mark on the appropriate scale indicating your level of endorsement for each common theme.

• Self-protection: "I fear my mate's response."

| Husband | Wife |
|---|---|
| ☐ Strongly Disagree | ☐ Strongly Disagree |
| ☐ Somewhat Disagree | ☐ Somewhat Disagree |
| ☐ Neutral | ☐ Neutral |
| ☐ Somewhat Agree | ☐ Somewhat Agree |
| ☐ Strongly Agree | ☐ Strongly Agree |

• Overprotection: "I do not want to hurt my mate's feelings."

| Husband | Wife |
|---|---|
| ☐ Strongly Disagree | ☐ Strongly Disagree |
| ☐ Somewhat Disagree | ☐ Somewhat Disagree |
| ☐ Neutral | ☐ Neutral |
| ☐ Somewhat Agree | ☐ Somewhat Agree |
| ☐ Strongly Agree | ☐ Strongly Agree |

• Rationalization: "It won't make any difference anyway."

| Husband | Wife |
|---|---|
| ☐ Strongly Disagree | ☐ Strongly Disagree |
| ☐ Somewhat Disagree | ☐ Somewhat Disagree |
| ☐ Neutral | ☐ Neutral |
| ☐ Somewhat Agree | ☐ Somewhat Agree |
| ☐ Strongly Agree | ☐ Strongly Agree |

• Misbelief: "Avoidance is the proper/Christian thing to do."

| Husband | Wife |
|---|---|
| ☐ Strongly Disagree | ☐ Strongly Disagree |
| ☐ Somewhat Disagree | ☐ Somewhat Disagree |
| ☐ Neutral | ☐ Neutral |
| ☐ Somewhat Agree | ☐ Somewhat Agree |
| ☐ Strongly Agree | ☐ Strongly Agree |

• Denial: "My mate never makes me angry."

| Husband | Wife |
|---|---|
| ☐ Strongly Disagree | ☐ Strongly Disagree |
| ☐ Somewhat Disagree | ☐ Somewhat Disagree |
| ☐ Neutral | ☐ Neutral |
| ☐ Somewhat Agree | ☐ Somewhat Agree |
| ☐ Strongly Agree | ☐ Strongly Agree |

# Three

**3**

# Avoiding Intimacy

# 12

## *Talk to Me*

A woman at a retreat described to me the personal characteristics of her parents and went on to relate a particular incident. Her father was very kind and considerate, but as the woman put it, "is the quietest man I know." This fact often frustrated her mother who really enjoyed a good conversation. On one occasion, her parents had decided to take a long trip by car, which meant spending a considerable amount of time together. In anticipation of this, the woman's mother resolved that she would not be the first one to speak once they were on their way. She would either casually observe the scenery or read a book until her husband initiated a conversation.

The trip began. With fortitude and dedication, the wife stuck to her plan. After *six hours* of noncommunicative behavior, in sheer frustration and no longer able to withstand the silence, she blurted out, "Are you never going to say another word?! How long can you go without carrying on a conversation?!"

The husband appeared shocked by his wife's comments. At first she thought that he might have been startled by just the break in the silence. But a further evaluation of his expression suggested she may have been mistaken. Her husband's look was more one of confusion than shock. Finally he uttered a response, "Why, I thought we had been talking." In his mind, they had been carrying on elaborate conversations ever since they embarked on their journey.

I do not want to take away from the seriousness of this situation. Neither do I want to belittle the frustration of the wife. Yet I chuckle every time I recall it. But it does illustrate a core deficit in marriage: the failure to talk. In healthy marriages, spouses share with one another. And talking is the primary way to do this.

## Intimacy Is a Twofold Issue

The term *sharing* has the connotation of giving. Spouses who share give of themselves to their partners. But when we look at how partners share in relationships, we find that sharing can actually take place in two entirely different manners and at two different levels.

Sharing takes place at both *quantitative* and *qualitative* levels. The quantitative level gives attention to how much and is not necessarily concerned with depth. The qualitative level identifies the depth or intimacy of the sharing. The theme of this book is: The natural tendency to be avoidant confronts spouses in every marriage. And this section delves even more narrowly into these common tendencies by examining specific interferences to intimacy. I want to help you understand what constitutes intimate sharing, the factors that prevent it, and the consequences of avoiding intimacy to a marriage. All of these issues are part of the qualitative level of a marriage, but I would be remiss if I did not differentiate between the two different dimensions of sharing.

Sharing is not an either/or situation. There is a definite two-dimensional quality to intimate relationships. A growing marriage requires a healthy dose of both quantitative and qualitative sharing. Let's see how you fare.

### Quantitative Sharing

The level of quantitative sharing that takes place between spouses is fairly easy to determine. We are looking at how much talking is done—not necessarily how well it is done. But "How much time does this couple spend together?" Whether in seconds, minutes, hours, days, weeks, or months, the time given to one another can be calculated.

In my work with couples, I usually ask them to answer a few simple questions. You may want to answer the same questions as a quick pulse-taking exercise. Do you notice any themes?

- How much time do you give to your spouse?
- Who or what gets more of your time?
- Of the things that compete for your time, where does your spouse fall on your list of priorities?
- In the midst of a hectic life, how hard do you try to make time to be together?
- Who usually initiates this kind of action?
- Is the way things are now an exception or the rule?
- Does it bother you if you and your spouse are unable to spend time together?
- Does it seem to bother your spouse when the two of you are unable to spend time together?
- How important is spending time together to you?

When dealing with couples regarding the quantitative level of sharing, I use terms such as *his, hers, theirs,* and *togethering.* In a healthy relationship, a balance is struck between the needs of the individuals and the needs of the relationship. It is when things get out of balance that difficulty arises. For example, there are several things that demand my time. Some of them are worthwhile endeavors such as my private practice, teaching and faculty responsibilities, writing, and involvement in a local church ministry. There are other activities that, though appearing less worthwhile, are still very important, at least to me. These are the things that I do purely for pleasure. I like to fish, run, and bike ride. All of the activities listed are the *his* in my life and marriage.

There is nothing wrong with any of the things that make up my his list. Whether the activities are either responsibilities or self-pursuits, they are basically healthy in nature. Nor is there anything wrong with my doing them. Jan has her own list of responsibilities and self-pursuits that make up the *hers.* There is nothing wrong with them, either. In fact, a marriage without a his and a hers can quickly become out of balance. Spending time together is the *theirs* of a marriage, the togethering of a marriage. If all that Jan and I were managing to do was the his and hers, our marriage would also be out of balance. Without all three, a marriage suffers.

Getting to know someone takes time. We remember that from our courtship days. There has to be personal investment. Though relationships change over the course of a marriage, the need for investing time does not. Maintaining a relationship is no less important, and no less time consuming, than getting one established.

Over the years, I have repeatedly heard the debate that rages between quantity time and quality time. I concur with the position that quality time is more important. But I strongly question whether there can be real quality time if there is not at least some quantity time; I do not think one can exist long without the other. Without an investment in the lives of the people we love, we lose touch. And one of the primary ways to demonstrate our investment and love is by giving them our time.

### Qualitative Sharing

The second dimension of sharing is quality, the difference between depth and what can be described as superficial. Quality sharing involves *real* talk. By making this distinction, it becomes evident that it is possible to talk and yet not really talk at the same time. The story of Steve and Connie, a couple I counseled, clearly illustrates this.

I had met with Steve and Connie for several weeks. We were meeting at Connie's insistence. Steve would have far preferred to be elsewhere. But when faced with an ultimatum, "go to counseling or I'm filing for divorce," Steve opted for what he described as the lesser of two evils. He was an engineer in every sense of the term, clearly a "just the facts, ma'am" kind of guy. Connie's chief complaint was that he was emotionally distant and remained peripheral to the entire family. "I want Steve to 'get in the game.' He always seems to be in a world of his own. I want him to get into our world."

In one particular session, we focused on personal needs and expectations for the marriage. One of the needs that Connie stated was for Steve to talk to her. Steve seemed frustrated, even insulted by Connie's suggestion that this was not occurring in their marriage. It was obvious from Steve's reaction that he and Connie were speaking two entirely different languages. "What do you mean we don't talk about anything of personal significance? Why, I talk to you about the weather all the time." Steve was not being facetious. He was dead serious.

I couldn't believe what I was hearing. I almost laughed out loud. Had Steve been looking at me, my facial expressions would have given me away. Fortunately, his eyes were fixed on Connie. When trying to emphasize the difference between superficial conversation and things of more depth, I frequently use the illustration of talking about nothing more significant than the CNN weather channel, a statement meant to push things to absurdity. Yet here was Steve citing it as an example of quality sharing! Steve and Connie were talking without really talking.

Spending time together is important. Although sitting together in front of the TV, going sailing, or spending a weekend at a resort are much needed respites for many of us, if you fail to converse about anything other than superficial matters, you are *relaxing*—not *relating*. The qualitative dimension of sharing deals with what you actually talk about during the time you spend together. When your talking is restricted to superficial matters, like Steve's discussion of the CNN weather channel, your relating is one-dimensional. A growing marriage requires a two-dimensional investment. It requires depth.

## Being Intimate

When I refer to *talk to me* in this book, I am addressing the important need for husbands and wives to relate at an intimate level. Being intimate has definite dimensional implications, both for individuals and relationships. For the individual husband or wife, it involves movement toward depth, moving away from the surface—the superficial yet protective pseudo image of yourself that is projected to others—to a more real and honest self. For the relationship, it involves movement toward closeness. Rather than keeping people at a distance, you let them into your space, to draw close. A healthy interdependency is developed.

Real talking is accomplished in several ways. One is by honestly sharing how you feel. Your feelings are extremely important, but they are also quite personal, so you have a tendency to protect them. Sometimes you even hide them from yourself. More often, you are aware of them but choose to hide them from your spouse. However, sharing how you feel—whether positive or negative—is a means of really talking that creates depth versus superficiality and fosters closeness versus distance.

Talking about how you feel involves sharing a kaleidoscope of emotions. You can share your fears, your needs, and your hurts or talk about feeling down, discouraged, and depressed and what seems to have made you this way. The mask is removed and insecurities displayed. These kinds of emotions are sometimes viewed as the dark side of feelings—things that could be viewed incorrectly by your spouse as personal inadequacies and deficiencies. But talking about feelings also involves sharing some of the positives, including your joys and what is causing them. You can let your spouse in on your secrets—your heart's desires, your dreams, and your aspirations. To talk about your feelings is to let your spouse into your life.

Another way to really talk is to share what you think. Beliefs, ideas, and values are examples of the thinking part of who you are. While they are not feelings, they may represent something that you have strong feelings about. And although thoughts are different from feelings, they can also be very personal. Choosing to share them is exactly that—a choice. It involves going beyond the superficial—remaining unresponsive or responding with "I don't know" or "I don't care"—to providing more depth.

Whether sharing what you feel, what you think, or a combination of the two, real talking requires that you be vulnerable. You have to be willing to open yourself up and take a risk, to be willing to share who you really are with your spouse, to make yourself known. And you also have to allow your spouse the opportunity to do the same, which requires listening.

Intimacy is the result of a cooperative effort. One spouse's sharing does not an intimate marriage make. But if both spouses are willing to really talk, the stage is set for a more rewarding marriage.

## *Not Always a Purist*

If real talking was that easy to do, we'd all be doing it. So there must be some complications. What I have found are some natural interferences that predictably get in the way of sharing with our spouses. In the rest of this section, I will identify the more common interferences, describe each one, and examine some of the ways to challenge, correct, and otherwise limit their effect on the development of healthy marriages.

Before delving more deeply into these interferences, I want to make one observation. Few of us are purists. Few of us are confronted with one—and only one—interference. It's not unusual to find several forms of avoidance to be familiar friends. But even though your particular problem may be more a blend of several interferences, one usually manages to emerge as the predominant interference. As we look at the five most common interferences to sharing, determine whether any are applicable to you and your marriage, but don't be overwhelmed. There are none you can't face and resolve.

# 13

# A Failure to Bond

For the first time in my life, I'm learning what it means to be a husband. That's what I want to be. I think I really am doing better. I just never understood what Debbie needed from me.

It may seem that Richard is giving a progress report on the changes he was making in his marriage. Actually, he had a far different intent. Had you been in the office, you would have noted the desperateness in his tone. Richard was actually making a plea for another chance in his marriage. But from all appearances, his plea was falling on deaf ears.

We were in the early stages of the counseling process. Seeing a marriage counselor had long been Debbie's desire, but Richard resisted. The decision to actually meet with a counselor came shortly after Debbie announced her decision to meet with an attorney to file for divorce. Though Richard and Debbie's relationship had been visibly deteriorating for several years, her decision finally pushed their marriage over the edge. She had changed the rules of their game, and they moved from chronic dissatisfaction to crisis. Far too frequently, it takes this level of intensity for couples to seek help.

I don't understand what Debbie's problem is. For years she has wanted more companionship. She wanted me to pay attention to her, to talk to her, to listen to her. Well, the first time I try to do something about it, what's she do? She just pulls away from me. I'm doing what she says she wants. And it's what I want. Why can't she accept that?

I don't think Debbie really knows what a good marriage is. I know she has said she wanted more. But I think she has only talked a good game. Since I've learned what true relationships are all about, I don't know if that's what Debbie has really wanted. She may have been willing to settle for too little also.

Richard saw himself as a new man. The crisis caused by Debbie's decision to see an attorney got the attention that ten years of her pleading had failed to do. Richard was now becoming a self-help authority. He was reading anything that might make him a better husband and improve his marriage—how to be more caring, more sensitive, a better sharer, a better listener, and a better lover.

I didn't doubt that Richard was trying to make some changes. But it was difficult to determine exactly what his primary goal might be—a true change in their relationship or preventing Debbie from leaving the marriage. There were some things about Richard that suggested he could be manipulative. Still, he was in a desperate situation—one that would tend to prompt insecurities in almost anyone. And ever since he had recognized the errors of his former ways, his behavior had been different.

Debbie also had concerns about Richard's motivation. But her concerns were stronger than mine. After all, hers stemmed from a ten-year history of marital dissatisfaction, where mine were the product of just a few weeks of counseling. Debbie questioned Richard's sincerity; might this be a case of his doing "too little, too late"? Debbie really didn't know where she stood in the relationship.

I was raised in a family where people talked to each other. We talked things out when there were problems. But it was more than that. We also talked about things that weren't problems. We talked about things that were important to us and about things that prob-

ably weren't. We just talked. There was a sense of being connected—a part of something. Mom, Dad, brothers, sisters—we all
just related to each other. I guess I didn't realize that people lived
any differently.

Richard did a better job of relating when we were dating. He
wasn't great. But he was better. After we got married, he just
stopped. He shut me out of his life completely. I got very little of
his attention. About the only time he wanted to spend any time
with me was when he wanted something. But he also shut me out
in ways other than time. He stopped talking to me about anything
important. And he never wanted to listen to me when I had something important to say. Our marriage became so artificial.

I felt so abandoned. Here I was married and yet I felt totally
alone. I longed for him to show he cared about me. But he didn't.
I told Richard how I felt, but it didn't seem to make any difference.
Things just continued as they were. There was no connection.
When I finally recognized the great void in our relationship, and
how other than convenience, there really wasn't anything holding
us together, I decided it was time to end the marriage.

I know Richard says that he now wants what I have wanted all
along. And he might. I just don't know if it's what I want any longer.
At least, I don't know if I do with him. I really don't know how I feel.
*There's just not much of us left.*

"There's just not much of us left." Of everything that Debbie said,
this one statement was the most descriptive, and the most revealing. It spoke about their marital history and their present. She and
Richard were at a turning point in their marriage. The difficulty facing them was that there was little on which to build.

There are consequences to everything we do. We discussed the
consequences of failing to deal with dissatisfactions in chapter 6,
how spouses erect emotional walls that block them from drawing
close or, if severe enough, even push them apart. Though the consequences of failing to talk and share have an entirely different
dynamic than the consequences of avoiding conflict, they are just
as significant. This significance was illustrated in the marriage of
Richard and Debbie, whose avoidance of intimacy resulted in a failure to bond.

## Pulling Together

I have already stated my position on the Lord's design for marriage. I believe that we are created with a yearning for closeness. We have a God-given desire to be in intimate relationship. This need for closeness is best met in marriage—not marriage as an institution alone, but also as a relationship. Marriage is intended to be intimate, not a static, perfunctory arrangement where highly specified and lifeless roles are methodically played out. It is a covenant between two people—a relationship that grows. It has life and passion. It is an ever evolving union entered with a commitment to lifelong, mutual investment. How can two spouses even think about approaching this level of intimacy without a willingness to talk and share? It cannot be done.

It is through talking and sharing—the act of self-disclosure—that closeness develops in a marriage. Without self-disclosure, the process of pulling together and bonding can neither begin nor continue. To help illustrate this concept, consider that people are much like onions: We have lots of layers. As we talk and share, gradually moving from one layer to the next, we let our spouses a little closer to who we really are (our core) and our relationship becomes more intimate. There is no other way for intimacy to occur.

Closeness of this magnitude involves a decision to trust. It also involves a decision to take a risk. It is risky business to be vulnerable and to open yourself up to someone else. But there is no other way—and the rewards are tremendous.

Sharing not only pulls a marriage together, it also establishes the bond that holds it together during the difficult times. Have you ever noticed how external crises seem to affect different couples in different ways? For some couples, these events are overwhelming and destroy the marriage. For others, there is almost the reverse effect. They not only survive the difficulty but emerge even stronger through the process. I believe that the reason for the different responses is found in what existed in the marriage before the crisis occurred. An analogy to this is a fine piece of china that happens to have a faint hairline fracture. Holding the china up to the light does not create the imperfection. It only illuminates what is already there.

The Lord's design for dealing with external crises is an intimate relationship. Closeness is the glue of a marriage.

## When Partners Don't Talk

Talking and sharing lead to an increasing level of closeness. When they don't happen, the opposite occurs. As in the case of Richard and Debbie, relationships do not remain purely static. There is movement in one direction or another. Though Richard seemed comfortable with the lack of connection, it was clear that Debbie was not. Over time, the difference in what each desired from the marriage finally created a crisis.

Spouses who do not talk and share are choosing to remain *emotionally closed*. This was what Richard chose. For some reason, emotionally closed spouses prefer maintaining distance in their marriages rather than striving for closeness. But there are always consequences associated with this decision.

The personal response style of spouses who choose to remain emotionally closed is destined to be superficial. They display no depth. They may be clearly avoidant as Richard was. Much of what frustrated Debbie was Richard's overt display of insensitivity to her needs. Others are more covert in their withholding. They may be pleasant and conversant. They may even be quite active socially, sometimes being the life of the party. But whether their basic nature is extroverted or introverted, the quality of what they have to share remains the same. Their talking revolves around surface issues, and the real self is never displayed.

There are personal implications as well for the other spouse in this type of relationship. They report feelings of loneliness, abandonment, and a sense of personal emptiness. These are not deep-seated, personal issues for which they need counseling; remember, we are created to be in relationship. Rather, these are natural responses to finding healthy needs for emotional closeness unfulfilled. Debbie expressed these feelings when she stated, "I felt so abandoned." Richard's individual decision also impacted Debbie's individuality.

The primary consequence of the decision to remain emotionally closed is relational distance. There is no connection between the spouses. They fail to bond—to pull together—and as a result fail to develop resilience. Instead, there is an emotional hole or void in the relationship. Debbie described this in her statement, "There's just not much of us left." When there is little *us,* there is little at all.

Whereas failing to deal with dissatisfactions creates a wall, failing to talk creates a hole. So when facing the "talk to me" issue in a marriage, we're not so much dealing with what happens between two people, but with what fails to happen. The entire emphasis of this book is a plea for husbands and wives to let each other into their lives. Let there be an us. When this fails to happen, there really isn't much left.

# 14

# Closed with Everyone

## Interference #1

The concerns that Peter and Deborah brought to counseling were not all that unusual: "We're not close." "We seem to have different needs." "I feel rejected and not cared for." "I need more intimacy from our marriage." "I keep waiting for things to change, but they don't." "I'm growing tired of the way things are." I had heard all of these complaints before. What may surprise you is that it was Peter who was more vocal. It was Peter who felt distant, who needed more closeness, and who was the natural sharer in the relationship. And it was Peter who was frustrated.

The perspective that places certain needs, behaviors, and complaints in tightly wrapped gender packages can be oversimplified and misleading. I believe that the differences in people, regardless of the multiple reasons for these differences, are of greater importance than the perceived differences between sexes. When it comes to looking at the needs of partners in a marriage, we are far better off recognizing that there is more that men and women share than there is that separates them. Safety, security, to love and be loved, to be appreciated—these are people needs, not gender needs. And differences should be determined by the specific needs of specific people—not by their gender. Peter and Deborah were an example of this.

> Deborah has always been a little reserved and distant. That was part of my attraction to her. I found myself in the pursuing role when we dated. That was a change from most of the girls I dated.
>
> I don't mean to imply that there is anything timid about Deborah. She's always been nice and sweet, but she's not shy. She can be assertive when she needs to be and is fine in social settings. But she just doesn't open up with me.
>
> I thought things would get better with time. But they haven't. (Pause.) I don't know what to say. It hurts. (Peter paused again.) I just need more from the relationship. I need for her to talk. And I don't understand why she can't.

Peter was outgoing and expressive. That made it easy to discern his level of frustration. His level of commitment to the marriage was also apparent. With statements such as, "I'm not here to end anything"; "I'm not quitting"; and "I just want things to change," it was also clear that Peter was not here to attack anyone. He just wanted to have a more intimate relationship with Deborah.

Throughout Peter's description, Deborah remained motionless. Her lack of expression was not motivated by fear. Neither was she feigning indifference to Peter's words. She was intently listening—hanging on to every word. Deborah was obviously concerned about what Peter was saying. But when he stopped talking, I was able to witness firsthand some of what he related. The room grew quiet. It was time for Deborah to share her perception of the marriage and to offer some kind of response to Peter's words, but her only response was silence.

I don't know how long the silence would have continued had I not intervened. I'm sure Peter would have again begun talking even if Deborah had not. But I was interested in hearing from her. So I asked her, "What do you think about what Peter is saying?"

> It's hard to know what to say. I understand what Peter is saying; I just don't have any answers. I know what he wants. And I'd like to

be more of a sharer. I'm just not comfortable with it. I don't know why. It's not Peter's fault. It's just always been that way. I've never been much of a sharer.

I'm a feeling person. I just don't like to share them much. They're personal and private. There are things I would like to say to Peter; I just can't. I like the way Peter shares with me. I guess I'd feel distant too if he didn't do that. So I understand what he's saying. But if he wasn't frustrated with the way things are, I'd be pretty content. It's comfortable for me just the way it is.

Deborah's response was candid, honest, and direct. Peter had been correct. There was no shyness or timidity in this woman. There was a hesitancy to speak, but this seemed to be related more to her confusion regarding why she was the way she was and her resulting inability to solve the puzzle that perplexed Peter. Deborah loved Peter. And she wanted to be more responsive to his needs. But sharing was uncomfortable for her. She didn't know why. It just was.

## Generic Means Everyone

Deborah tended to keep things to herself. This wasn't because Peter was an unusually difficult person with whom to communicate. Neither was it a response to something he had done. Deborah's hesitancy was in spite of Peter's having been a loving, committed, and emotionally open spouse throughout their marriage. Deborah's reluctance was totally of her own doing, something she brought into the marriage as opposed to developing it within the relationship.

It is the historical and pervasive nature of this tendency to be emotionally closed that makes it generic and helps to distinguish it from other forms of interference. Deborah did not discriminate among people. In her mind, all were equal, including Peter. No one was any more privileged or any less special. She kept her feelings to herself and did not share with anyone.

The operative word here is *anyone*. In my questionnaire, I assess the presence of this interference by asking partners to either endorse or reject the following statement: "I have always been a very private person when it comes to sharing how I feel." Those who strongly agree with this statement are suggesting their tendency to be intimate. Disagreeing may not guarantee that they are emotionally open, because some other interference may block their attempts to be intimate. But they are at least denying the presence of a generic or pervasive tendency to be emotionally closed.

## Problems with Trust

To assume that most emotionally closed individuals do not experience emotions would be faulty. Admitting to being emotionally closed is not the same as admitting to having no feelings at all. Most emotionally closed people do have feelings—strong and deep feelings. They just view these thoughts and feelings as expressly personal and private. Deborah alluded to this when she said there were things she would like to say to Peter, but she just couldn't. This is a characteristic that could be said of several types of interferences. The difficulty of many emotionally closed people is not in having feelings, but in sharing what they hold to be private and personal.

At the core of this tendency to be avoidant is a lack of basic trust. Though an issue for the marriage, it is not one that arose because of the marriage. Like the tendency to avoid itself, it was brought into the relationship. Realizing this can be quite disturbing for the partner who desires more from the marriage. Later in our session, Peter described his frustration over Deborah's lack of trust this way.

> I don't deserve this. I've never deserved this! If I had done something—anything—to betray Deborah's trust, I could understand her hesitancy. But I haven't. I just don't understand why this is so difficult for her.

Deborah was concerned about Peter's frustration. But she had no answers for his questions. She was also confused: "I don't know why I have difficulty trusting people." Deborah was being truthful with Peter. With generically closed individuals, it is sometimes difficult to identify when and where the tendency to be closed began. As with Deborah, it's just always been that way. In other situations, the emergence can be charted, beginning with an incident or a relationship.

Unlike some other interferences to intimacy, the tendency to be generically closed seems to offer no automatic answer or standard rule suggesting why people are closed. It varies with individuals.

Another characteristic associated with being generically closed is that this interference frequently does not stand alone. Perhaps the difficulty in identifying a consistent cause of this form of interference is because it is frequently coupled with a variety of other forms of avoidance. For example, a mate who is generically closed may also have the problem of having learned the wrong things in a bad home environment, which created the difficulty with trust. Or a mate who is generically closed may also have a problem with appropriate role perceptions that helped create the difficulty with trust. Some of this may be more of a "what came first, the chicken or the egg" scenario. But one thing is certain, it is not unusual for interferences to come in pairs in this situation.

For some generically closed mates, marriage offers the first (and possibly the only) experience with a non-superficial relationship. Though it may appear meager to a frustrated marital partner, and though it may pale by comparison to what could potentially be, time and relational stability have teamed together to offer an otherwise closed mate the opportunity to make forays into risk taking. Gradually, a level of trust has been built up, and for this reason, many mates who respond that they are emotionally closed also report that they are satisfied with their marriages. This was Deborah's response. Though Peter really wanted more from their relationship, Deborah was experiencing as much closeness as she ever had. And she was basically happy with the way things were—"If only Peter could be satisfied."

## *Influencing Readiness to Share*

What will bring change to a marriage where one of the partners is generically closed is influenced by the choices made by the closed mate and the level of true commitment to the relationship. If the generically closed mate chooses to deal with this interference, and if he is committed to both the marriage as an institution and as a relationship, the task is simpler. But usually change also involves a degree of readiness on the part of the closed mate. Change in a relationship can be a cooperative effort between mates. What is the posture of the frustrated mate? What can be done to either encourage readiness or aid the adaptation of a closed mate's behavior? These questions stress that even the disappointed mate has responsibilities in the change process.

In the apostle Peter's first letter to fellow Christians, there is a passage that stresses a theme we would all do well to remember. In talking about how we influence those with whom we have contact, Peter suggested that what we do can have significantly greater influence on another person's behavior than what we say.

> In the same way you women must accept the authority of your husbands, so that if there are any of them who disbelieve the Gospel they may be won over, *without a word being said*, by observing the chaste and reverent behavior of their wives.
>
> 1 Peter 3:1–2, italics mine

I do not believe we need look at this passage to try to argue the case for or against submission in marriage. That wasn't Peter's point. The focus of this Scripture is clearly on winning converts and not on encouraging mates to be more open in their sharing within their marriages. But there is a theme in this Scripture that can serve as an example of an alternative means of influencing a mate.

Peter suggests that there are ways of influencing a person other than telling him what he ought to be doing, whether our telling is occasional or frequent. (The latter is known by other terms such as *harassment, coercion,* and *nagging.*) People can be influenced "without a word being said" simply by our behavior. In most instances, people already know what they ought, should, or are supposed to be doing. Our reminders are not all that helpful and usually serve more as something to be resisted by the nonconformer or as a means of venting our own pent-up emotions (and meeting our own needs) than as a true reminder.

Telling closed mates that they need to be open and self-disclosing if intimacy is going to develop in their relationship is okay on occasion. But most mates are smart enough to comprehend this message after they have been informed once or twice. To persist in telling them what they already know can result in resistance and an even greater tendency to be emotionally closed—the opposite of what you want. There is a better way to behave—a way that not only can bring greater calmness to you but also can increase the possibility of your mate's becoming more intimate.

It is far better to focus on your own behavior and talk about your own needs than to repeatedly tell a mate what he ought to be doing. Your influence will come from your own openness and not from any attempt to force your mate to do anything he is not ready to do.

### 1. State your needs and desires directly.

"I need . . ." is one of the healthiest phrases that can be spoken in a marriage. It is also one of the least frequently utilized. In far too many marriages there is a hesitancy to talk about personal needs. Sometimes this is due to a fear of appearing weak or emotionally needy. At other times, talking about needs is equated with begging and is accompanied with the attitude, "If you have to ask for something, that takes away from the meaningfulness of what you get."

Being able to state needs in a healthy way has several positive influences on a mate who is generically closed. First, it takes away the element of blame. The emphasis is shifted from the mate who is not measuring up to your needs; this relieves his feeling of being under attack and allows for less resistance and defensiveness. Stating needs also gives your mate an opportunity to demonstrate sensitivity in the marriage. Roles are identified: You have a need; he can respond to it. There is something inviting about a mate who needs something from you. Lastly, stating needs brings clarity by eliminating confusion regarding expectations. Confusion often exists because our communication consists of either weak signals (failing to clearly state needs by offering hints, giving nonverbal cues, or making statements with hidden meanings) or magical thinking (making assumptions such as "If he really loved me, he would know what I need"). Stating "I need" eliminates confusion.

### 2. Do not pursue.

Once your needs are clearly stated, you need to back off and give your mate some space. This requires a delicate balance. You do not want to pursue him, but neither do you want to pull away. Your goal is to take a healthy stand.

Pursuing behavior is anything that unnecessarily crowds or presses your mate and is obtrusive and demanding. Nagging is a good example of pursuing behavior. Though the very mention of a need results in some mates being falsely accused of being naggers, truer discriminators of nagging are frequency and intensity. If I use correct words, but repeat my statements of need on a daily basis, the mere frequency of these words is obtrusive. Or if I allow pent-up frustrations to explode in an emotionally charged assault, the intensity of what I am saying overrides any appropriateness in the content of my words.

State your needs directly and appropriately. Be cool, calm, and collected. Be sure that you are heard and then back off. Be patient. Give your mate both space and time. Giving your mate emotional space allows him an opportunity to demonstrate sensitivity. Giving him time allows him to do so at his own pace. Change can be gradual, and time enables the process of change to occur.

Backing off is easier when your emotional eggs are placed in more than one basket. Do not expect your marriage to meet all of your needs. Seek out and develop other relationships and interests. This does not mean that your marriage should be neglected—that would be an example of pulling away. But remember that a healthy marriage practices his, hers, and theirs forms of behavior. Strive for a balance. It makes backing off a more achievable goal.

### 3. Model what you want.

Scripture frequently refers to consequences for our behavior. That is what is meant by "you reap what you sow" (see Gal. 6:7). This principle of reaping and sowing has great application in marriages with generically closed mates. If you want to reap more sharing in your relationship, you had better sow it.

Modeling what you want serves two functions. First, we learn a great deal through observation. Talking to your mate and sharing what you feel and think is a form of teaching. You are demonstrating behavior to your mate that he hopefully will embrace and emulate. Modeling sharing behavior also invites a mate to participate by encouraging him to come alongside and join you. The relationship begins to look like a safe place. After all, you are sharing. What's to stop him?

### 4. Do not become resentful.

Resentment, hostile attitudes, cold responses—these are not endearing qualities that attract mates or invite closeness. These and similar behaviors and attitudes push them away. Your aim is to provide a safe environment characterized by calmness and acceptance. For a closed mate to begin to open up requires that he take a risk, something he has comfortably avoided doing for most of his life. Your being resentful will only make the process that much more difficult. Staying calm is easier said than done, but here are some things that will help.

- **Acknowledge your anger.** It is normal to become frustrated and angry. Just don't let it lead to resentment. Deal with your anger. Admit it, face it, even share it with your mate. Denying its presence only pushes it down and allows it to fester. Get it up and get it out to some form of resolution.
- **Remember that you have a plan.** Things are not as you would like in your relationship, but you are not helpless. You are not idly sitting by, passively allowing your marriage to meander along a dissatisfying course. You have chosen to deal with your relationship in a positive, responsible, and constructive manner. Though there are no guarantees that what you are doing will improve your relationship, you are doing your best. Being assured of this should bring a heightened sense of calm in times of doubt.
- **Recognize your mate's limitations.** There is something to be said for accepting the fact that your mate has limitations. This attitude of acceptance is not to be interpreted as license for your mate or a rationalization by you. Neither of you needs to live in denial. Ideally, things need to be changed. But you must realize that husbands and wives have differences, that being different is not the same as being deviant, and that even if a mate does commit to dealing with some of the interferences

to developing intimacy in your marriage, it does not mean that there will be a total, complete, or instantaneous change. At some level, you may need to settle for something less than ideal.

Accepting and making allowance for differences in a mate is a difficult task. A growing marriage possesses several forms of love. One of these is romantic love. It is characterized by passion and celebrates our "sameness." (There is seldom friction in areas of likeness and agreement.) A growing marriage also possesses agape love. This is a deeper, nondemanding, and selfless love. Agape love makes allowances for the shortcomings in a marriage and is demonstrated in your response to your mate's differences.

Recognizing limitations and accepting differences are difficult to discuss. We tend to make gross generalizations that, when applied to the actual characteristics of a specific marriage, prompt questions of appropriateness and application. Do you love unconditionally? Do you accept the person but reject the behavior? Is that the same as loving unconditionally? I don't know that we can make absolute statements regarding acceptance. Individuals must answer these questions for themselves. There may be a balance to be struck, but there is a place for a healthy portion of agape love and acceptance. Without agape love, it is doubtful that a mate who is already hesitant to share will venture out. And without agape love, your own level of frustration will only continue to heighten. Accept your mate's uniqueness and build on that.

- **Invest in other areas of the marriage.** You want a more intimate marriage, and you want more sharing from your mate. But in the midst of these legitimate desires, you need to keep your marriage and your life in proper perspective. There is far more to life than marriage. And there is more to your marriage than the element of sharing. Strive for balance.

Just because the talking and sharing aspect of your relationship is not going as well as desired does not mean that the other areas of your marriage should be neglected. The true level of intimacy in your marriage is dependent on how well you are investing in several dimensions, not just one. Continue to talk and listen at whatever level your mate is willing to interact. Continue to spend time together, both as a couple and in social groups. Continue to deal with dissatisfactions. Continue to pursue joint recreational activities. Continue to prioritize your sexual relationship. And continue to prioritize your spiritual development, both as an individual and as a couple. In short, continue to invest in your marriage in its generic sense. Do not let limitations in one area totally disrupt the marriage as a whole.

These suggestions have been offered as aids to the mate who desires a change. They are not exactly wordless, but the heart of Peter's admonition is found within them. Do not place your focus on telling your mate what he ought to do, or even stooping to demonstrations of strength and power. This is not an area where coercion is very effective. Instead, choose to influence your mate through your own admirable behavior. Let him know what you need. Model the behavior. And then invite him to join you by demonstrating your love. Provide both a safe environment and the opportunity for change. Influence is more productive than control any day.

# 15

## Closed with Mate

**Interference #2**

Brian and Marty were a picture of contrasts. Brian was rather large and Marty was petite. He was intense; she was calm. He was loud and boisterous; she was reserved. And Brian was overbearing in his presentation, at times almost intimidating, whereas Marty spoke with well-paced self-control. When Brian would launch into one of his emotion-laden discourses, Marty did not wither away or shrink back. She merely waited for Brian's demonstrative outburst to run its course and then calmly and directly responded to his accusation.

The ease with which Marty handled Brian's form of directness suggested that it was not altogether new or foreign. She had seen it all before. Whether she had always been calm while in the line of fire or this was a trait she had acquired as a result of her marriage to Brian, she presented an image of someone who was not easily flustered. Like the palm trees that survive hurricane and gale-like winds in tropical areas, Marty could ride out storms of a personal nature.

Brian and Marty had both agreed that it was time for some counseling. Neither of them was pleased with where their relationship seemed to be headed. But during this first session it was Brian who professed to being the most dissatisfied. He described Marty as aloof

151

and distant. No matter how hard he tried, he just couldn't get close to her. Sprinkled throughout his description of their marriage were phrases such as: "She's distant and closed off from me." "She's nice enough. Even cordial. But she doesn't seem to really want to have anything to do with me." "She doesn't talk about anything important or share any part of her life with me." "There's no passion, no life coming from this woman. Just coolness."

The session ended with Brian and Marty agreeing to complete some tests and to meet with me later individually. There was little resolved during that first session, but that was not surprising. The initial session is a time for gathering information, hearing complaints, beginning to establish a working relationship, and agreeing on a structure and plan for the counseling process. It is also a time for me to begin formulating hypotheses about the marriage. As I began to do this, there were several things that just didn't make sense.

Brian forcefully presented the case that Marty was an extremely emotionally closed individual who could not open up in the marriage. Using words such as "could not" placed emphasis on Marty's capabilities, suggesting that she was lacking in some way. Though Marty had not denied Brian's accusations, neither had she admitted to them. There seemed to be more to this situation.

Marty impressed me as different from the stereotypical generically closed mate. She was not as guarded. I wondered if Brian's assessment was completely accurate. Maybe it was true that Marty was avoiding being intimate with him. But was this a matter of capability? Were we dealing with an issue of could not or would not? Was there more going on in this relationship? To this point, I only had questions.

I knew I would have the opportunity to meet with Brian and Marty individually before resuming any joint sessions; mates are sometimes more willing to disclose sensitive information privately. I also knew I would soon have the benefit of some test results. I believed that this tangible information might help clarify my confusion and at least provide me with further questions for our upcoming individual sessions. It was in examining the results of one of these tests, the Marital Interaction Inventory, that my confusion began to disappear.

The Marital Interaction Inventory was designed to allow mates to give graduated responses (five choices from strongly agree to strongly disagree) instead of forcing a true or false selection. This graduated response style allows for a more accurate description of a relationship. But there is something to be said for seeing things from a black and white vantage point. I wanted a caricature of the marriage and wondered what kind of marital profile would emerge if Marty's answers were converted from the graduated responses to either true or false. This kind of manipulation would not pass for good research, nor would it be a good assessment. But it might help in developing and challenging some hypotheses.

Below are some of Marty's responses converted to true or false. I selected those statements that best lent themselves to providing a caricature of Marty's view of the marriage and arranged them cohesively. What emerged proved to be quite revealing.

The first set of statements identified what Marty was doing. Her responses confirmed Brian's description of her as avoidant. She was not sharing anything personal with him.

I refrain from sharing my feelings with my husband. [True]
Dreams, goals, beliefs—these are the kind of things that I share with my husband. [False]

The next set of statements provided me with some crucial information. Marty's responses supported my suspicion that she was not generically closed. Marty reported a history of being open and sharing.

I have always been a very private person when it comes to sharing how I feel. [False]
I'm not good at sharing my feelings with anyone. [False]

As is frequently the case, the elimination of one question prompted the rise of several others. Marty was open and sharing with others but not with her husband. What made the difference? The next set of statements helped me to rule out two possible culprits.

I don't believe it is the feminine thing to share. [False]

I have many things of a personal nature I'd like to share with my husband. [True]

Marty was not confused about her role in the marriage, nor did she lack a desire to share with her husband. Though these responses helped me to rule out some possible interferences, they did little to rule in Marty's reason for choosing distance over intimacy. Her responses to this final set of statements began to shed light on their relationship.

Everything new I have learned about my husband has pleased me. [False]
I can state my feelings without my husband getting defensive. [False]
My husband accepts me for who I am. [False]
I have some needs which are not being met in this relationship. [True]

Marty appeared capable of sharing. She simply chose not to. And the reason for this decision was somehow related to Brian's behavior. According to Marty's responses, she was no Deborah. But neither was Brian a Peter.

## Distinguishing between Generic and Specific

Remember Peter and Deborah? Deborah was emotionally closed in the relationship, but her behavior had nothing to do with Peter. He had been a model husband. Deborah was generically avoidant—sharing with anyone was difficult and had always been that way. So she maintained a comfortable distance in all of her relationships, including her marriage. This was not the case with Marty and Brian. Marty was admittedly closed in her relationship with Brian, but this tendency to maintain a safe and comfortable distance in her marriage appeared to be more of an exception for Marty, not the rule. This was not the usual way she related to others. And Brian appeared to be less than a model husband. The differences between these two marriages clearly illustrate the differences in these two interferences to intimacy.

It is important to differentiate between the *generic* and the *specific* forms of being emotionally closed. The theme for the generically closed mate is, "It's uncomfortable for me to share with *anyone.*" This is in direct contrast to the theme for mates who are specifically closed: "It's uncomfortable for me to share with *my mate.*"

Mates who choose to be specifically closed are discriminating. They are quite capable of being emotionally close and intimate in relationships and choose to be with some people. They just don't choose to be close with their mates.

Why is it that some mates will share their feelings openly with people in general but withhold in their marriages? There are several lesser explanations. One concerns gender and role issues. Some husbands interpret their role as the head of the home to include showing no sign of weakness. They fear that by sharing feelings their position of authority may be weakened. Consequently, they remain stoic and aloof. Another explanation relates to the significance placed on marriage itself. Commitment intensifies a relationship because it increases the level of expectation and the consequences of potential loss. There is more to lose if a marriage sours than with any other relationship. It is one thing to lose the respect of a friend or to be rejected by an acquaintance. But to lose the respect of, or to be rejected by a mate is a far more serious matter. With more to lose, more caution may be exercised.

Occasionally, we find specifically closed mates who are avoidant because of these lesser reasons, but they are in the minority. Usually when this anomaly is found, it is as a by-product of the relationship itself and is historical. Something specific has happened in the marriage, either an incident or a pattern, that has caused a mate to shut down. The emotionally closed mate has learned that his or her partner is not to be trusted, and the decision to be distant is a decision for safety.

## Home Is Not a Safe Place

When mates choose to share with others—to be self-disclosing and to develop intimate relationships—but refuse to do so at home, the overwhelming reason for this discrimination is self-preservation. Specifically, closed mates invariably feel that home is not a safe place. When confronted about their selective use of sharing, the following justifications are frequently offered:

> It's not safe to share with my mate. He doesn't accept me.
> It's not safe to share with my mate. He attacks me.
> It's not safe to share with my mate. He uses what he learns against me.
> It's not safe to get close to my mate. I just end up getting hurt.
> It's not safe to get close to my mate. He is unreliable and lets me down.
> It's not safe to get close to my mate. He just uses and abuses me.

As Marty began to share her story, I found that her statements of concern were no different from the justifications related to me by countless others. She also found home—and living with Brian—to be unsafe.

> Brian says that he wants closeness—for us to be a team. And he says that he wants me to share my feelings and thoughts with him—to confide in him. But he doesn't. Not really. Every time I have tried to do just that—to be a part of a team or to share what I felt or thought—it ended up with him getting upset.
>
> Brian cannot stand for me to feel something that he does not think I should feel. If I do, he just discounts it. "You don't really feel that way." "How in the world could you feel like that?" "You shouldn't feel that way." The fact that feelings aren't necessarily right or wrong—that they just are—doesn't make any difference to Brian. If he doesn't understand them, or if he doesn't agree with them, he doesn't accept them. And then he gets upset and rejecting.
>
> It's the same way with my thinking. If my opinion—whatever I may be thinking—is in any way contrary to the way he is think-ing, Brian gets upset. What began as a discussion becomes a debate. He does not rest until he changes my mind. He takes every-thing so personally. He believes we have to be in consensus on everything. In his mind, that's what it means to be a team.
>
> I've learned a lot by living with Brian. I've learned to keep my mouth shut. I keep my feelings and thoughts to myself. Why go

through needless pain? Brian is self-centered, controlling, insensitive, non-accepting, defensive, and uses things against me. Do I need to say anything else? There is no point in trying to be close. He won't let it happen. No matter what he *says*, it's what he *does* that keeps me distant. And unless something changes, that is where I intend to stay. *It's just safer that way.*

## Reasons for Change

Marty was a smart woman. She was also creative and adaptable. But this is true of most specifically closed mates—they are survivors. They learn what is safe and what is not. And from this experience, they develop a means or plan to bring calmness into their lives that involves maintaining a safe distance. Not from everyone but only from the one who has a history of hurting them—their non-accepting, insensitive, rejecting, unreliable mate.

For closeness to develop in a marriage, there must be sharing between the mates. This is something that is obviously not taking place when a mate chooses not to disclose in a marriage. For this interference to intimacy to be changed, the specifically closed mate must be willing to change his or her behavior, and doing this will require taking a risk.

Because these mates have adapted their behavior to bring safety into their lives, doing anything different involves renewed risk and goes against their survival instincts. Why should they once again risk hurt and pain? For them to take such a risk, they must be given a reason. There must be a tangible change in the relationship that brings the potential for safety. Short of this change, it is not likely that the specifically closed mate will give up the calm of distance for the renewed chaos of self-disclosure.

I have dealt with the issue of changing these historical relationships in *A Change of Heart: Restoring Hope in Marriage* (Baker Book House). I do not intend to rewrite that book here, but I will summarize what must occur in this relationship. The specifically closed mate must have some indication that the future will be different from the past, and this comes from a genuine reconciliation.

Reconciliation is the biblical means of healing a relationship. It involves four steps that are characterized by the following statements: "I'm wrong"; "I'm sorry"; "I'm changed"; and "I'm committed." When a mate such as Brian genuinely embraces his role in the marital failure (I'm wrong), expresses remorse for the pain that his behavior has caused (I'm sorry), begins to change his inappropriate behavior (I'm changed), and commits himself to constructively dealing with his marriage (I'm committed), a lot of history seems to wash under the bridge. Genuine reconciliation offers the Martys in these relationships the opportunity to once again take a risk. They can give up the safety of distance for the intimacy brought by self-disclosure.

# 16

## *Faulty Learning*
### Interference #3

"Nobody ever did it in my family," said Dennis, an attendee at a seminar I was conducting. We were discussing intimacy in marriage and the role each mate's family plays in developing the ability to share. Dennis was referring to the failure of any member of his family to talk about how they were feeling—ever!

None of the adults in my family ever talked about feelings. Not my grandparents, not my uncles, not my aunts—none of them. They always seemed to have a good time when we got together for family gatherings. You know, like at Christmas and Thanksgiving. Everybody seemed to like everybody. But the conversations were always light and jovial. I heard all those family stories. You know, what Uncle Fred and Aunt Joan did when they were kids. Seems like I heard some of those stories several times. We always had a lot of fun, but no one talked about anything of an emotional nature.

Things weren't any different at home where it was just us. Don't get me wrong. *I came from a good home.* Mom was always there for my brothers and me. I never questioned whether she loved us. But she was always in that motherly role. You know, supportive, encouraging, and always ready to give advice. She knew exactly what we ought to do. But she never really talked with us. It was always to us. I never heard her talk about feelings.

It was the same when someone else wanted to talk. On those rare occasions when my brother or I started to share something of a personal concern, Mom didn't know what to say. It just made her really uncomfortable. Dad was even worse. He was a quiet man and hardly talked at all. He certainly wasn't going to talk about how he felt about something.

Nope. In my home, I just didn't see much of what you're describing. And it really had an impact on how Cindy and I related in the beginning of our marriage. I didn't know what she wanted from me. It has taken a long time for me to overcome home and to learn what to do.

## A Good Home

Dennis was probably accurate when he said, "I came from a good home." There was no question in his mind that he was loved and that home was a secure environment. There was no bickering between his parents. Both were consistent, stable forces in his life. And though his family had not been wealthy, all of Dennis's basic needs had been provided for. A good home is delineated by the concept of stability. In that regard, Dennis's assessment was true. He had come from a good home. He had just not come from a nurturing home.

The difference between a good home and a nurturing home is found in how well emotions are handled within the family. What is the frequency and ease in which things of an emotional nature are dealt with? Is conversation meaningful or superficial? In Dennis's home, there was no ease with emotions, and significant conversation was avoided. Whether by conscious design or unintentional and automatic, only things of a superficial or functional nature were discussed. Family members had feelings—they just did not share them. That became a family rule.

In a nurturing home, a different rule exists. Feelings are important, and family members are allowed to recognize, accept, and share what they think and feel. There is a freedom to disclose what is going on in their lives, whether joy, pain, or confusion. These are shared—

and they are heard. Moms, dads, and siblings talk about what is important, and the result is closeness within the family.

We learn a lot at home. Some of what we learn is functional, such as how to use proper manners, how to clean our rooms, how to prepare a meal, and how to mow the lawn. Other things that we learn are more complex such as values, roles, and how to relate to people. Some of our learning is intentional. It was no accident that I learned to tie my shoelaces; I was taught to do this. But some of what we learn at home is unintentional. Dennis's parents had no intent to teach him to be superficial in relationships. They thought they were doing a good job in their parenting, and they were. They probably did the best they knew how. But in spite of their intent, Dennis learned how to be avoidant, and he carried this learning over into his marriage.

The theme that underscores this interference to intimacy is, "I never really learned to share my feelings with anyone." Though there are other institutions and events in life that influence what we learn in childhood, there is no influence greater than the home. Another seminar couple, Allen and Kari, contrasted the differences in homes as each reflected on what they had learned in their families. There was a sense of pride in Allen's voice as he stated, "I learned to be open. That's just the way it always was there." Kari's comment contained just as much emotion as Allen's. Hers, however, was not from pride, but determination. She was making it clear that the past did not have to dictate her future. "I learned to keep things to myself. There was too much tension created when I did anything else."

It is Kari's response ("I learned to keep things to myself") that represents faulty learning. It was not what her parents intended to teach, but it was what she learned. It underscores the truth that not everything learned at home is good—and not everything is intentional.

## Home and Learning: Models and Environments

Dennis emphasized what he had failed to learn at home and stressed the concept of modeling. He never learned to share because he never saw it modeled or demonstrated by the adults in his family. But there is more to learning than the presence or absence of adequate role models. Kari illustrated this difference when she spoke of learning to keep things to herself. This was an example of contextual learning. Our difficulty is not always failing to learn. Sometimes the real problem is learning far too well—the wrong things. Either one represents a form of faulty learning.

Every family has its own set of rules. Some rules are formal, expressed and talked about. They may not be the real rules, but they are the stated guidelines for the family. For example, the formal rule in a home may be that no one may bring food into the living room. When little Johnny brings food into the living room, his mother reminds him of the family rule. Johnny ignores her and begins to eat his food. Mother then tells him again what he is and is not allowed to do. He continues to ignore her prompting. After several more incidents of Johnny's ignoring his mother, she finally loses all control and screams at him. He looks at her, lets out a sigh of disgust, and stomps off with his sandwich in hand. Now, the formal rule in this home is "you cannot bring food into the living room." But the real rule is that "you can bring food into the living room until mother has told you five times what you already know, turns red in the face, and screams." We live by the real rules, not the formal. Families function best when there is little difference between what is formal and what is real.

There are also informal rules. These rules are not stated and may even be unrecognized or denied. But they exist nonetheless. In Dennis's home, there were formal rules about personal responsibility. Each family member was taught to carry his fair share of the work load. There were rewards for being responsible and consequences for being irresponsible. For the most part, everyone followed the rules, and the household ran smoothly. There were also informal rules in Dennis's home. "Don't share anything of a personal nature because it makes others uncomfortable" was an informal rule. No one ever stated this rule, but its presence controlled the family's behavior. This rule was never violated. Keeping personal things to themselves kept everyone comfortable, and no one wanted to rock the boat.

We learn to survive home. Survive is a harsh word, but I want to convey that we learn to exist within whatever situation or context we find ourselves. And within this context, we learn to bring as much calmness to our lives as possible. Usually this means that we quickly learn the family rules and abide by them. Failing to abide by these family rules can result in a great deal of personal discomfort—something we are intent on avoiding. That is what Dennis did. He learned to deal with the stress and pressure created by any attempt at sharing by ceasing to share.

Contextual learning can take many forms. I met with Terry, who explained what he learned at home this way.

> Home was a disaster. My parents were crazy. They weren't really crazy. They just acted that way. They were always drinking and arguing. Sometimes they reminded me more of children than adults. My sister and I always seemed to be in the way of their having a good time. We were burdens. At least, that's what they communicated.
>
> We couldn't really depend on them for much of anything. As we got older, we mostly took care of ourselves. We couldn't go to them with problems or needs. They were too caught up in their own problems to be interested in ours.
>
> I remember the day when I made the decision that I didn't have to be like them—not that I was. It finally hit me. They were crazy! If they wanted to continue to be crazy, they could. That was up to them. But I didn't have to be. That decision was up to me. It was then that I began to disconnect from my family. I was barely a teenager so I had no choice but to physically remain a part of the family—even if only peripherally—until I was old enough to go off to college. But emotionally, I left home that day in early adolescence.

Home had proven to be unsafe. There were several ways that Terry could have responded. He chose to disengage from his family. Disengagement is a normal developmental action for children. But Terry chose to emotionally leave home prematurely—at a much earlier age than most children—and for far more protective motivations. Considering Terry's context, his choice was one of the healthiest things he could have done. But this choice carried with it several predictable consequences. Children who disengage early from their family of origin are highly self-reliant, independent, self sufficient, and resourceful. After all, they learned that others could not be counted on, and relying on others only brought disappointment. So they learned to take care of themselves, to meet their own needs, and to accomplish goals in the most difficult of circumstances. A final consequence is hesitancy to trust—this also only brought them pain.

Premature disengagement brought sanity to Terry's life. But the survival strategies that brought him sanity as a child—self-reliance, independence, self-sufficiency, resourcefulness, and mistrust of others—only interfered in the establishment of intimate relationships as an adult. He learned well, but his learning was faulty. As an adult, the discomfort came with his attempts to trust and to establish an interdependent relationship.

Throughout the years, I have heard many examples of unsafe contexts and the faulty learning that was the result. One man described a mother who was pushy. "You couldn't give her an inch without her taking a mile." What did he do in order to bring calmness to his life? He learned to erect a strong defense. He'd stay away from home. When at home, he avoided conversations, always kept his feelings to himself, and constantly remained on his guard. And at the first sign of pressure from his mother, he would launch an all-out counterattack (after all, the best defense is a strong offense). How does he relate to his wife? In much the same manner.

I have heard adult clients tell stories of being rejected and discounted as children. Children who are raised in families where little time is taken to deal with the things that seem important to them—children who are passively rejected—begin to feel that they too are unimportant. What do they do? They close up emotionally and learn to keep things to themselves. And those who find their feelings discounted—"You don't really feel that way"; "It's wrong to feel that way"; "You should feel differently"—begin to feel inadequate, and they close up too. The scenarios are endless. But once a survival strategy is learned, it becomes an important part of a child's, and later an adult's, life.

These are all examples of learning, not necessarily the result of modeled behavior, but learning nonetheless. Each individual learned to protect himself from pain, to bring safety to his life, through avoidance. The particular threats confronting these individuals and the specific strategies developed to avoid these threats may have been different, but the goal and motivation was the same—safety.

## Putting Away Childish Things

Scripture records, "When I was a child, my speech, my outlook, and my thoughts were all childish. When I grew up, I had finished with childish things" (1 Cor. 13:11). Other translations use phrases such as "put off," "put away," and "I gave up childish ways" when describing Paul's distinction between childhood and adulthood.

Paul's intent in writing these words was to draw a contrast between lesser and best, between partial and whole, and between incomplete and complete. The best, the whole, and the complete represented love. Everything else—a prophet's work will be over, tongues will cease, knowledge will vanish away—were representations of the partial, "and the partial vanishes when wholeness [love] comes" (1 Cor. 13:10).

Being aware of Paul's intent, it is easy to understand why he would choose the differences between childhood and adulthood as one of his analogies. There is a distinct difference in the quality of life in these two stages. But in real life, though there are many things that do change as we progressively mature to adulthood, there are still others that we fail to relinquish (put off, put away, or give up). A more accurate paraphrase of 1 Corinthians 13:11 that reflects real life is: "When I was a child, I spoke as a child, I behaved as a child, and I thought as a child. Though much of this childishness changed as I journeyed through the stages of life toward adulthood, there are some things that I learned so well, I continue to do them though I am now an adult."

We do not put off all that we learned as children. At least, we don't do so automatically or easily. We all learned to survive home and childhood. Whether we were fortunate—our parents were good, our homes bordered on the ideal, and outside events and influences were all positive—or whether our circumstances were less than fortunate—parents, home, and outside events were disappointing and tragic—we developed strategies for bringing some sense of security into our lives when things were chaotic. These strategies, not necessarily modeled and frequently unintended, were developed on our own. They have protected us so well during our years of vulnerability that they have become old friends. As such and ignoring what society marks as the passages of life, they have transcended one developmental stage to another to become a part of who we are today.

Sometimes the strategies we learned served the important role by enabling us to survive in a less than ideal context. But now they interfere with the development of intimacy. A little later in this book, we will look at some of the ways we can face and resolve these interferences to intimacy in marriage. It will involve recognizing what health is, identifying our own personal strategies that interfere with our achievement of health, understanding where these strategies came from, and possibly even gaining an appreciation for what might have been a real lifesaver during a difficult period of time.

We cannot change our past. But we can change the impact it has on our present. A childhood does not have to haunt an adulthood. However, attitudes of "that's the way I was raised"; "my behavior is the result of what I experienced in childhood"; and "that's what I learned to do" can mistakenly lead to feelings of justification and a decision to accept things as they are. But we do not look to the past to embrace license; we look to the past to understand the present and to better determine what we have to change. The past does not automatically disappear, and change does not come easily. But it can come. It begins with a decision for health, a choice that only you can make.

# 17

# Role Misperception

**Interference #4**

"Marvin is a millionth-generation farmer." This was Joy's introductory statement as she began to describe both her husband and her marriage. A specific caricature came to mind with Joy's statement. This caricature was enhanced even more by the tone of her voice. Joy sounded frustrated and exasperated. It was obvious that there was something about Marvin that she found displeasing. Joy went on.

Marvin loves it. Farming is his passion. He gets in the fields with his tractor and feels as though he's close to heaven. It's all he knows. With the exception of some short-term factory work, it's all that he's ever done and all he wants to do.

Part of what makes farming so enjoyable for Marvin is the connection it provides him with his family. He shares the land with his father and brother, so he spends a lot of time with them every day. I don't doubt that it's hard work. But I sometimes think that they spend more time talking and running around together than they do working.

I could handle the farming. And I don't really mind him spending time with his family. If he could only fit me into his life. That's what really bothers me. Marvin doesn't come in until late. And when he does, he just wants to sit in front of the television and relax. I want to talk, to listen to him talk, to communicate. Marvin doesn't. And he sees no need for it. I don't know if it's that he can't or won't communicate with me. Either way, I feel totally abandoned in this marriage.

Marvin doesn't see where it's his role to relate in his marriage. His parents didn't do that. And neither did their parents. Marvin believes that that's the way it's supposed to be, and he doesn't want it any different than it's always been. Well, I need more!

Joy's problem wasn't with Marvin's passion for farming per se. It was with his lack of investment in the marriage, both functionally and emotionally. He could have farmed until his heart's content if only he could demonstrate a like passion for his marriage. But he did not. He invested little energy, quantitative or qualitative, in the relationship. There was no time, no depth, and from Joy's perspective, there was nothing at all. And she was tired of this.

What about Marvin? How did he see it? *Was* he the millionth-generation farmer Joy described? Or did he have some redeeming qualities? He consented to meet with me if it would help Joy. This gave me an opportunity to have my questions answered.

All in all, Marvin seemed pleasant enough. He said a few nice things about Joy—how she cared about him, the children, and their marriage. He applauded her for being a hard worker and for recognizing that farming was a difficult life. But when it came down to how he really saw things in his marriage, and in relationships in general, it became increasingly clearer that Joy's description of her millionth-generation farmer was fairly accurate.

I think we've got a pretty good marriage. I know it's a little rough on Joy with my being a farmer. I wish I could be home more—to be there for her—but I can't. Work interferes. But it's not that way with just us. That's the life of a farmer. All of the other marriages that we see are the same way. In our community, husbands and wives just don't spend much time together.

Marvin was heavy into roles. From his perspective, there was a prescribed and acceptable role for a husband and a prescribed and acceptable role for a wife. The fact that such a prescription resulted in a marriage where "husbands and wives just don't spend much time together" didn't seem to make much difference. After all, that was the way things were supposed to be.

## Not My Role

Marvin did not state directly that he did not believe it was his role in marriage to relate to his wife, but he might as well have. All of the indirect signs were there. Marvin was content with his marriage. He cited work as an interference to spending time together, but that seemed okay with him. After all, in Marvin's community, husbands and wives "just don't spend much time together."

Because the manner in which he related to Joy was directly tied to his perception of roles, in essence Marvin was saying that sharing was not his role. I attempt to measure the interference to intimacy that comes from role misperceptions with this statement: "I don't believe that sharing your feelings is the masculine/feminine thing to do." Those spouses who somewhat agree or strongly agree with this statement believe that relating in marriage is not a part of their role. Those spouses who somewhat disagree or strongly disagree with this statement believe the contrary.

The decision to embrace a role that eliminates the responsibility for sharing in a marriage usually originates in an extreme interpretation and acceptance of one side of the nature versus nurture controversy, the age-old debate regarding what exactly influences our behavior. Are we programmed to behave in a certain manner because of biological and genetic predispositions (nature), or are we born as blank slates and our tendencies determined by the environmental influences that impact us (nurture)? An extreme belief in either of these positions can significantly interfere with the intimacy level of a marriage.

*Men Are from Mars—Women Are from Venus* is a popular secular book that strongly endorses the nature position of this controversy.[3] In his book, Dr. John Gray asserts that men and women are innately so different that it is as if they are from different planets. Though Dr. Gray's position does not promote any type of creationism, he claims our predisposed tendencies are nonetheless beyond our control. We are destined to behave in a certain manner. He suggests that accepting the reality of these basic differences will go a long way toward lessening the frustration that can emerge between men and women in relationships.

When Christians engage in the nature versus nurture controversy, we can argue either of these positions even more convincingly because we are armed with God's authority. A Christian argument for the nature position can be found in works of authors such as Gary Smalley. Though these authors endorse creationism instead of evolution, the practical emphasis is again on our predisposition and largely innate nature. Men were created with one nature, women with another. They also suggest that accepting this fact is our best recourse.

Whereas the nature position can be represented by the statement, "God created me to be this way," Christians can also argue for the role of nurture. Those who endorse the influence of nurture would state, "God designed men and women to live in a specific fashion." This latter emphasis is not on any genetic or innate predisposition but on an identifiable and appropriate lifestyle. This position asserts that it is God's will that men and women relate to one another in a prescribed manner.

I'm not here to argue for or against either position. Probably there is some truth in both, and some error. My real concern with nature and nurture rests with the extremes to which the positions can be pushed. Any position, if pushed to an extreme, can become exclusive in nature.

What if it is true that men by nature are less adept at dealing with how they feel than are women? Does that mean they cannot deal with emotions at all? Hardly! But sometimes even the notion that men or women are meant to do or not do something can be used as an excuse. When you get down to the specific aspects of whether men and women should openly deal with dissatisfactions or talk about what they think and how they feel, it seems errant to push our beliefs about both nature and nurture to such an extreme to suggest that men and women are categorically different. There is more that we share in common than separates us.

## Justification

In my initial conversation with Marvin, his rationale for failing to relate in his marriage was linked to nurture. He related to Joy the same way he had observed his parents relating, and his parents' parents before them. Even the other marriages with which he was familiar related in this manner. Perfunctory, matter-of-fact, minimal personal investment—these had been the behaviors that Marvin had seen modeled. With such a cloud of witnesses, how else was he to define his role as a husband and Joy's role as a wife? In Marvin's mind, this was the way it was supposed to be.

The problem that accompanies these misperceptions is that they lead to an attitude of justification. Marvin may have found sharing too uncomfortable and therefore something he would like to avoid. But that's okay because it wasn't really his role to share anyway. Either because of genetics or cultural mandates, he had an excuse.

I like to fish. But I haven't always fished. I went fishing a few times when I was a young boy, but I was raised in a metropolitan area where fishing was not easily accessible. Nor was it seen to be as much a part of a person's life as it is where I now reside. So my fledgling interest was quickly replaced by other activities. I was in my thirties when the dormant desire began to reemerge.

My interest and skill have both increased over a period of several years. I began as a real novice with a left-handed (I am right-handed), hand-me-down fishing rig and one lure. I was fishing with my brother-in-law Ken who was quite accomplished in the art. After fishing for several hours, he chided me for repeatedly using the same lure. "If they're not biting on that one, switch to another." His suggestion made perfect sense to me, but I was there to relax. It made no difference to me whether I caught anything or not. I was enjoying the process. I caught no fish that day—I was "skunked." But that was of little significance. As I remarked to Ken, "The phone didn't ring one time while I was on the lake."

The passage of time has brought some differences in my fishing. I no longer fish with hand-me-down gear. I can now choose from over half a dozen state-of-the-art rigs. Progressing from the meager beginning of one lure, I now routinely carry as many as three tackle boxes containing everything imaginable for the up-to-date fisherman. And I seldom get skunked.

But some things have not changed with the passage of time. I still enjoy the process. The addition of equipment has not changed my pleasure. If anything, it has enhanced it. It allows me to practice the art in a better way. I still do not have to catch anything in order to have a good time. I am there to enjoy the process of fishing, not necessarily to catch fish. The phone still does not ring while I am on the lake, which makes for a relaxing day. And Ken is still a better fisherman than I; he is a natural. This is not likely to change. I am becoming a good fisherman, and I will probably become even better. But I will never practice the art as well as Ken.

What does any of this have to do with husbands and wives, men and women, and dealing and sharing? Simply this. Anyone can learn to fish. Whether male or female and whether possessing natural talents or not—it doesn't make any difference. Some are genetically predisposed to be better than others or are raised in an environment where it more naturally becomes a part of their lifestyle, but these are issues that differentiate between better and best—not between can and can't. There is no exclusiveness in fishing—for any reason.

The same can be said of dealing and sharing. Even if you want to cling to some rationale of differences between the sexes on either genetic or cultural grounds, you can only acceptably use these positions to differentiate between better and best—not can and can't. I know many men who share well. And I know many women who deal well. These are not mutually exclusive behaviors, and neither are they mutually exclusive roles. When exclusive roles are embraced, it is more a case of won't, not can't. There is no legitimate justification for avoidance by identifying with any role.

## A Problem for Men and Women

We are quick to think first of men when exploring the tendency to misperceive roles and to embrace an attitude of justification.

Though there is some gender connection, I find men and women alike stumble over the issue of roles. For example, the role misperception most common among men involves their perspective about talking. Sharing thoughts and feelings are commonly seen as feminine, not masculine. After all, you never heard "the Duke" talk about his feelings. For women, the misperception more commonly involves feelings of anger. Some believe it is inappropriate for women to deal directly with frustrations—it's just not ladylike. Not only are these attitudes inaccurate, they also interfere with what husbands and wives should be doing in relationships.

Men are very capable of sharing, and women are very capable of dealing (behaving assertively). Even making these pronouncements seems to support the traditional stereotypes. Therefore to avoid being stereotypical, I will also add that men are very capable of dealing with anger and women are very capable of talking about how they feel.

In healthy, growing relationships, men and women equally take part in both dealing and talking. They face their dissatisfactions, and they share what they think and feel. This is not an issue of gender or roles. Men can, and need to, relate in their marriages. The same is true of women. Anything that stands in the way of this—whether a learned behavior, a genetic predisposition, or an indoctrinated view of the roles of men and women—needs to be challenged and resolved.

## A Helpful Metaphor

What stopped Marvin from sharing in his marriage was thirty-plus years of cultural experience. Undoubtedly, there was some faulty learning involved in this interference to intimacy. But the primary blockage was Marvin's perspective of what was right and wrong. Marvin embraced a prescribed role. He was, as Joy described, a millionth-generation farmer. And in his mind, that meant there was no need for any of this relational stuff for which Joy so desperately cried out. Marvin felt justified in his avoidant behavior, and until there was a change in his belief and position, there would be no change in his relationship.

What do you do when you are faced with the task of dealing with a millionth-generation farmer? I figured we should talk about farming, so I asked Marvin to talk to me about what he does. Having been raised in a metropolitan environment, my knowledge of farming is limited. My question prompted a complete change in Marvin's countenance. I had touched his passion. It was easy to see how Joy could sometimes feel as though she were competing with a mistress.

Marvin was articulate and precise. I found his description of both farming in general and his specific activities to be fascinating. Occasionally I would ask a question but only in an effort to bring clarification. He seemed to have all the answers.

After several minutes of listening to Marvin talk about the present art of farming, I asked him to tell me about how it used to be. After a moment or two of contemplation, he said that the advancements made in farm machinery were the greatest single influence on farming. "It's changed everything." Marvin shared some stories he had heard about the "good ole' days" and conceded, "Frankly, I don't hanker for a return of the good ole' days. I'd far rather farm with my tractor than do it the way my grandfather did. He had to use mules."

"You know, Marvin," I told him, "farming has a lot of heritage and tradition in it. As much as you like farming, I'd think that you'd want to preserve some of that. Why don't you just go ahead and use mules instead of your tractor? I mean, that's the way it was done for a lot of years. Don't you think that would be kind of nostalgic?"

Marvin chuckled and just shook his head for a moment or two. Then he responded, "Yeah. Right! And why don't you just walk to work." We both had a good laugh. I then began to get to the point of my inquiry into farming.

"Farming has been around for a lot of years," I said. "There are probably some things about it that will never change. There are others that have—and for the better. It used to be that everyone used mules, horses, cows—any animal that could pull a plow. But like you said, you wouldn't want to trade your tractor for an animal—no matter how much a part of tradition that may have been.

"The institution of marriage has also been around for a lot of years. There are some things about it that will never change. But like farming, there are others that have—and for the better. Many people used to view marriage only for its functional value and assigned the partners highly prescribed roles. There wasn't much emotion or closeness involved. The wife was responsible for the children and everything inside the four walls of the house. The husband was responsible for providing for his family and for everything outside of the house. Sex was perfunctory, communication was minimal, and companionship was not an issue. But things have changed.

"Many people now see marriage as a relationship—something that offers a deeper sense of caring. Husbands and wives relate to each other. They talk, they listen, they spend time together, and they even blend some of the traditional roles by each taking responsibility for bringing in some of the family income, performing household duties, and taking care of the children.

"Farming and marriage aren't so different after all. Both have changed. And to make either one of them work, you also have to make the necessary changes."

There was no applause when I finished my statement. Marvin didn't stand up, shake my hand, and exclaim, "Wow! Now I get it." But he did listen. He sat for a few moments in silence. But the silence appeared to be productive. Marvin didn't get defensive, he just soaked it in.

You never really know how what you do in a session will ultimately affect a couple. As it turned out, what happened that afternoon proved to be a beginning. There was a lot of Marvin that continued to be Marvin. That was okay, because there was a lot about Marvin that Joy loved. But over time, Marvin gradually began to make some changes. After all, he no longer viewed marriage as he had for over thirty years. It, like farming, had changed.

# 18

# *Unrecognized Need*
## Interference #5

Pam, Greg, and I were meeting for a joint session, but it had taken a while for us to get to this point. In the beginning, Pam came to counseling alone. She had invited Greg, but he chose not to attend. "If I go, I want to see the counselor by myself" was his response. Greg did not seem to be as interested in working on the marriage as in presenting his side. Pam had no problem with Greg's presenting his perspective on things, but she also had a good grasp on reality. If she waited for Greg to initiate counseling, it would never happen. So she scheduled an appointment for herself.

At that first session, Pam shared a story of marital deterioration. Though gradual, encompassing nearly fifteen years of marriage, it had also been continual. She rarely remembered times in their marriage that could be described as disappointment free. Pam's themes were familiar: "I want a companion"; "I want to be cared for"; "I'm tired of being the one who brings life to this marriage!" Pam cried as she shared some of the history of their marriage and enumerated her complaints about Greg. She appeared to be able to express emotion freely. She ended her story by describing herself as a woman starved for affection.

I vacillate between frustration and shame. It makes me angry when I think of what I'm not receiving in my marriage. But then I feel ashamed for needing anything at all from Greg. Why can't I just be a rock—like him?

Pam did not spend all of her time discrediting Greg. She made some very favorable statements and spoke of Greg as "a nice guy"— the type of husband that many women would be happy to have.

Greg's ultra responsible. He doesn't mistreat me—at least in the way that we usually think of. He's predictable and reliable. For these I am thankful. But it's never been his doing bad things that has caused problems between us—it's his failure to do some good things.

Greg is basically nonresponsive to me. I can't get him to talk with me. I can say something directly to him, and it will just lay there without him even acknowledging that I said a word. He hears me— I know he does. He just doesn't respond. That drives me crazy!

This craziness had lately brought out some of the worst in Pam. She shared that their relationship had degenerated into a cycle. There would be a day or two of arguing, which primarily consisted of Pam expressing her discontentment and Greg finally being goaded into responding. The marriage would then enter a cooling-off period. During this time Pam and Greg would each maintain their distance. After a couple days of silence one of them would break the ice and a few days of civility would follow. During this phase, they might even pretend that things were good between them. Then another fight would erupt and the cycle would be repeated.

This part of our marriage is difficult for me to talk about. (Pam paused and took a deep breath.) There are some things that I have begun to do when I get angry with Greg that I'm not proud of. He makes me so mad. I say and do some things that I shouldn't. I've even slapped him. It didn't used to be that way. It's gotten worse lately. I'm just getting so fed up. That's what has brought me to counseling. Something has to change.

Greg thinks that all of *our* problems are really *my* problems. I used to think he might be right. But I don't believe that anymore.

I don't want too much. I think that a lot of other women would be frustrated too if they had to put up with what I have to.

## *Emerging Discontent*

Though Pam had been discontent for quite a while, she had not always been vocal about it. In the earlier years she would smile, pretend the subtle rejections didn't hurt, and hope that the marriage would get better on its own. But now most of her hope was gone. This loss of hope, coupled with an increasing vocal stand regarding her dissatisfactions, had changed the atmosphere at home. There was now intensity in their relationship. And Pam's discontent had prompted discontent in Greg.

As long as I suffered in silence, everything was okay with Greg. Once I began expressing my dissatisfaction, he became unhappy. Greg likes things calm and peaceful. He doesn't like waves of any kind. My talking about being unhappy rocks his boat.

Greg can't figure out what I'm so upset about. From his perspective, there's no reason for me to be unhappy. What really infuriates me is Greg's attempts at analyzing me. He can't see the real problem being either him or the marriage. It's got to be something within me. So one week he claims the problem is my low self-esteem. Supposedly, I'm so consumed with personal unhappiness—with being dissatisfied with who I am—that I can't be satisfied with him. The next week he states that my problem stems from the poor relationship I had with my father. Because of the rejection I got at home, Greg believes that I'm hypersensitive to even his slightest imperfection. Finally, he reasons the real problem is my refusal to forgive him for something he did in the past. Greg really hurt me several years ago. That's true. But now he figures I just haven't truly forgiven him for that.

Greg's list of reasons for *my problem* makes me sound like an emotional and spiritual invalid. My self-esteem may not be the greatest, my dad wasn't the greatest father in the world, and I sure didn't like what Greg did to me ten years ago. But none of these things are controlling my life today. And none of them address what Greg is doing right now in our marriage. It's what he's doing today—or better yet, what he's not doing—that frustrates me.

Pam was certainly dissatisfied. She wasn't ready to end her marriage, but she was definitely ready to see it changed. I wondered where Greg was in all of this. Was the marriage as Pam had described it? Was Greg as disinterested in a companion relationship as Pam claimed? She indicated that Greg was willing to meet with me on an individual basis. Would he follow through? I extended him a no-strings-attached invitation to meet with me. His coming would not commit him to marital counseling; nor would it be taken as an admission of guilt. It would merely be an opportunity for Greg to state his perspective on things.

## A Difference of Opinion

Greg came for an individual session. He was everything that Pam had reported him to be. He was nice, quiet natured, and appeared very responsible. And he saw the problem as Pam's.

> I've given this a lot of thought. I'm not the greatest communicator. I'd be the first to admit that. I don't talk much. I don't listen well. I'm not much of a sharer. And I certainly don't respond to some of the things she asks me. That's all true. But none of that's the real problem. It's my wife.
> Pam has low self-esteem. She shouldn't, but she does. And her relationship with her father was terrible. I feel like I've paid the price for his rigidity for years. And there's some stuff in our past— some stuff that I did that I'm not real proud of—that I don't think Pam has let go of. As long as she clings to the past, there's nothing I can do that will be enough. If she'd just take care of these things, everything would be okay.

It is always interesting to talk to husbands like Greg because they don't seem to have a clue. Greg said things like, "I'm not much of a communicator"; "When it comes to deeper things, I'm not much of a sharer"; and, "I don't seem to need the things she needs." Yet after all of these admissions, he seemed to make no connection between the basic emotional needs of a relationship, what he is and is not doing, and Pam's dissatisfaction. Greg still asserted that the problem was Pam.

Contrary to Pam's feelings, and with the exception of times when she was particularly upset with him, Greg was content with the marriage as it was. If only Pam could be happy, everything would be just fine. This other-focused position is common for husbands like Greg. They frequently defer to their spouses as if to say, "I'm doing however she is doing. It takes very little for me to be satisfied. As long as she's happy, I'm happy." They are comfortable with emotional distance in the marriage. It is their spouse's discomfort with the void, however, that creates the tension in the relationship. Greg's discomfort came from Pam's and not from anything within him. So, if she could only be content, everything would be fine.

When asked what they want to see happen in the marriage, these husbands again respond from an other-focused perspective. "I just want her to be happy." This has a nice sound to it—almost caring. But it is really as much a self-serving attitude as a demonstration of genuine concern. These husbands are well acquainted with the rewards of a contented spouse—"no hassle for me." And they are also aware of the consequences of discontentment. For purely personal reasons, these husbands prefer the former.

Greg was nice, and he was responsible. He had many of the qualities that bring stability to a marriage. But the more Greg talked, the clearer it became that Pam was correct. Amidst all of Greg's positive points were some significant lackings. And it was these things that he did not do and, possibly, things that he did not need that presented difficulties for this marriage.

## The Theme

A theme began to emerge in my session with Greg. He and Pam had different needs when it came to closeness. At least they had different needs regarding sharing. Pam had both the desire to share and to have it reciprocated, but Greg appeared to need neither.

Greg is not the first spouse to report a lack of desire when it comes to sharing. I assess the presence of this kind of interference with the following statement in my relationship questionnaire: "I have many things of a personal nature to share with my spouse." Some spouses respond to this statement with a great deal of affirmation—"I strongly agree. I have a lot to share with my spouse." Obviously, these spouses are different from the Gregs in the world. Mates like Greg strongly disagree with this statement, indicating that they simply have little to share—and correspondingly, have little need to share.

In the purist sense, these spouses are deficient. They lack sensitivity to situations and to others. Though sometimes they recognize their personal insufficiencies, frequently they do not. They are unknowingly insensitive. In addition to insensitivity, they also share an uncanny ability for creating frustration in their spouses as the following examples demonstrate.

> Jim wouldn't know an emotion if it bit him on the nose. He doesn't have any himself and he sure doesn't recognize them in someone else. This infuriates me.

> John is so dense. I told him I needed him to talk to me—to share what was going on inside his head. I explained that I felt distant and needed something to connect with. Do you want to know what his response to my cry for help was? "Do you want to watch *Batman*?" He wanted to know if I wanted to sit down and watch a video movie with him! How dense can you get?!

> Tracy is a good mother. But she's just not what I need in a wife. I need someone who will talk to me about what's going on inside of her. Not all the time. But at least some of the time. That's not what I get. The depth of Tracy's sharing is limited to the activities of her day and the achievements of the kids. When I get frustrated with this and voice my concerns, it's as if I'm from a parallel universe. She has no comprehension of what I'm talking about.

There are few people who experience only this type of interference. Usually there is something else contributing to their difficulty to share. But even though there may be some other interference—the presence of some natural discomfort whether specific or generic, a history that includes some faulty learning, or some confusion regarding what is and is not an appropriate role—the predominant theme continues to be personal deficiency. The desire to talk about what's going on in the life of the mate—whether inside or out—on other than a superficial level just isn't there.

## Whats and Whys

How does the premise of being created for intimacy and the reality that some spouses have little desire for closeness and sharing mesh? I do not totally understand why the needs for closeness and sharing vary so drastically among spouses. There are all kinds of theories that offer explanations, which are summarized in the nature versus nurture controversy. On one end of a continuum would be the nature theories that state that the differences between people are in their genes. We are all born with temperaments that will control our lives regardless of outside influences. On the other end of the continuum are the nurture theories that emphasize environmental influences instead. These propose that because of a self-protective reaction to a less than ideal family environment, the need to share or to be close has been either blocked, extinguished, or driven so deeply into the psyche that it is unrecognizable.

Whether the true answer to the inequity that exists between spouses involves something other than these two extremes, or is a combination of both, or will be different for each individual is difficult to say. However, though I do not understand all there is to know about need, I do understand what it means to be committed. Commitment to a relationship means doing what is in the best interest of the relationship regardless of personal comfort—and personal need. If sharing, listening, and talking are the types of activities that help build a relationship, then a committed spouse will strive to do these—regardless.

## The Intervention

With this particular case, I decided that the traditional approach of meeting with Pam and Greg jointly might prove counterproductive. Rule number one when dealing with a distancing spouse is never pursue him. Greg was an emotional distancer, and I felt that trying to involve him in joint counseling at this time would be an act of pursuing. Not wanting to violate the cardinal rule, I suggested that Pam and I continue to meet on an individual basis. Greg was told that he was free to return whenever he felt the need but, at least initially, his involvement was not required. Greg was surprised by my suggestion, but being a nice guy, he cooperated fully.

Pam and I began looking at some of her personal issues and also restructuring her participation in the marriage. For instance, rather than placing all of her emotional eggs in one basket, Pam was encouraged to establish some additional support networks. She began developing some friendships and participating in group activities without Greg. Pam was also encouraged to pursue personal interests—some alternative passions. As a result, she began biking, something she had always wanted to do. Finally, she was encouraged to invite Greg to participate in some together-time activities with her. But rather than selecting activities that were dependent on his participation, she planned those that could be done without him. If he refused to be a part of her plans, she could go anyway.

Through a series of activities, whether designed as a healthy investment in herself or a planned restructuring of how she related in her marriage, Pam successfully backed off from Greg. Her withdrawal was neither motivated by spite nor vindictive. In fact, it wasn't really much of a withdrawal at all but more of a standing still. Instead of pursuing Greg and working alone to keep togetherness in the marriage, she was determined that there be cooperation. It was like playing tennis. From here on out, volleys would have to take place. Pam's serves would have to be returned, and Greg would even have to take his turn serving, or the game would not be played. For Pam, the marriage had changed. But what about for Greg?

## The Change

Pam and I had met for several counseling sessions over the course of three months. Occasionally Greg would ask her what we were talking about in our sessions. Pam would simply reply, "We're working on some of my personal issues." She would then go on about her business. Though Greg was unsure of what was actually being discussed in the counseling sessions, of one thing he was certain—things were different at home.

To my surprise, both Greg and Pam came to one of the scheduled appointments. Sensing some confusion on my part, Greg was quick to volunteer an explanation: "I invited myself along." I ended up spending most of the scheduled time with Greg instead of Pam. He talked about his confusion regarding where his marriage was going. And he talked about his concerns. He still saw the problems as Pam's and once again stated her probable difficulties. But this time, I challenged his assumptions.

"You know, Greg," I told him, "I think there is some possibility that what you're suggesting are issues for Pam. She probably could have better self-esteem. There are some issues there with her father. And maybe she still has some remembrance of the past. But I don't really think any of these are the real problem here. I don't hear Pam asking for anything that isn't legitimate. The real question seems to be, What stops you from giving her what she needs?"

Changes were beginning in how Pam and Greg related. But it's important to understand what was occurring and why. Greg was changing because of what Pam was doing. But for this to be good change would depend on motivations. Healthy change focuses on doing what's best and not necessarily on trying to change others. An emphasis on changing others as a primary goal can lead to manipulation. Pam needed to make several changes in her marriage, but she needed to make them for herself, for her own personal health. It was not healthy for her to take sole emotional responsibility for the relationship, though she had persistently done so for years. She needed to do something different, and the change was good for her. But it also proved to be beneficial for her marriage. By backing off, Pam created the possibility for a change in Greg as well.

We cannot control the behavior of others. Nor should we try to. But what we do definitely influences them. That's what happened in this situation. For years, Pam's effort to get Greg involved in the marriage had maintained his emotional comfort level. Her pursuing served to keep him connected with little or no effort on his part. Pam's new behavior changed all of this. Without her constant efforts to keep him connected, Greg began to sense a void. It probably wasn't anything like the void Pam had sensed throughout the years of their marriage, but at least his own level of discomfort had been raised. Having gotten Greg's attention, we now had a place to begin our joint effort.

What followed for Greg was a gradual awakening to the needs of relationships in general and of Pam in particular. In and out of session, Greg began to genuinely listen. He listened to my description of health. He listened to my assessment of how his marriage had not measured up. And he listened as Pam talked about feelings and articulated her needs. But more importantly, for the first time in over fifteen years of marriage, Greg heard what was being said. Greg was beginning to realize that things truly needed to be different. This brings us back to where we began this chapter.

## Turning the Corner

Greg, Pam, and I had been talking about some events that had occurred since our last appointment—things that had not gone well. Sometimes you can get so caught up talking about events that you miss the real issues. That seemed to be happening here. Our meeting was shaping up to be one of those no-win sessions where a couple seems content to remain stuck in a never-ending cycle of attack and counterattack. After several minutes, I interrupted Pam and Greg.

"You know," I told them, "it's clear to me that you both care a great deal about each other. But somehow this caring breaks down in the translation. It just isn't getting communicated. I think you're both fighting over the same issues that originally brought you in." To Greg I said, "You want Pam to be happy," and to Pam, "You want a companion."

I told Greg, "You have expressed your concern for Pam. And you've stated your desire for her to be happy. Obviously, you cannot assume complete responsibility for her happiness or unhappiness. But you can do your part in making this relationship work. When Pam tells you that she needs a companion and that she does not see how she can be happy in this relationship without one, what does that mean to you? What are companion behaviors and what are you doing in this marriage?"

The office grew silent. Pam knew the conversation had shifted and was now between Greg and me. She would not interrupt. Greg also knew it had shifted. I waited for his response.

"I guess she needs for me to communicate with her, to let her into my life and to show that I'm interested in hers," he said.

"How exactly would you do that?" I asked.

"I could start by sharing what I'm feeling, whether it's good or bad. And I could respond to her like she's been asking me to do."

"That sounds like it would be a good start. But what do you think it communicates when you aren't willing to do these things?"

"I guess it says that I don't care very much."

"That's not how you really feel toward Pam. But that is what gets communicated. Somewhere in this marriage, you need to start doing the things that communicate how you really feel."

It was later in this session that Greg told Pam he was sorry. Pam was a little confused by these words. She had not heard them very often in their marriage and thought at first that he was referring to an incident that had occurred a few days earlier. But she could tell by his expression that he meant something more. She inquired, "I don't know if I understand what you're saying. What do you mean?" There were tears in Greg's eyes and his voice broke as he spoke, "I'm sorry for not being there for you for all these years. I'm going to do better."

There was more operating in Greg than merely unrecognized need. But that's the way it is with most of us. Seldom is there one and only one interference. Still, a lack of need was the predominant interference for Greg. Though there were other components, Greg had not been uncomfortable with the emotional distance that had existed in his marriage. But this session marked a true turning point for Greg and Pam. Greg's discomfort did not all vanish. Nor did he become significantly more insightful. He still missed some of Pam's subtle emotional cues, things that others might more easily perceive. But he had turned a corner. He saw the needs in his relationship and was finally committed to investing more in his marriage. With Greg's resolve and Pam's cooperation, the two of them began working toward becoming companions, not just roommates.

# Reflecting on the Motivation to Avoid Intimacy

Dealing with intimacy avoidance involves whats, hows, and whys. The whys are our motivations, which can be quite different for couples and even for the individuals in a particular marriage. The themes for the common interferences to intimacy—why spouses do not talk and share—are listed below. For the purpose of this exercise, each theme has been placed in the form of a statement. As you evaluate your own avoidant behavior, ask which of these lie at the core of your decisions. What interferes with your being closer to your spouse? Two scales are provided offering an opportunity for both partners to respond. Indicate your level of agreement of each statement.

• Emotionally closed with everyone: "It's uncomfortable for me to share with *anyone*."

| Husband | Wife |
|---|---|
| ☐ Strongly Disagree | ☐ Strongly Disagree |
| ☐ Somewhat Disagree | ☐ Somewhat Disagree |
| ☐ Neutral | ☐ Neutral |
| ☐ Somewhat Agree | ☐ Somewhat Agree |
| ☐ Strongly Agree | ☐ Strongly Agree |

• Emotionally closed with mate: "It's uncomfortable for me to share with *my spouse*."

| Husband | Wife |
|---|---|
| ☐ Strongly Disagree | ☐ Strongly Disagree |
| ☐ Somewhat Disagree | ☐ Somewhat Disagree |
| ☐ Neutral | ☐ Neutral |
| ☐ Somewhat Agree | ☐ Somewhat Agree |
| ☐ Strongly Agree | ☐ Strongly Agree |

• Faulty learning: "I never learned how to share."

| **Husband** | **Wife** |
|---|---|
| ☐ Strongly Disagree | ☐ Strongly Disagree |
| ☐ Somewhat Disagree | ☐ Somewhat Disagree |
| ☐ Neutral | ☐ Neutral |
| ☐ Somewhat Agree | ☐ Somewhat Agree |
| ☐ Strongly Agree | ☐ Strongly Agree |

• Role misperception: "It's not my role (God's design, culture, genetic) to share."

| **Husband** | **Wife** |
|---|---|
| ☐ Strongly Disagree | ☐ Strongly Disagree |
| ☐ Somewhat Disagree | ☐ Somewhat Disagree |
| ☐ Neutral | ☐ Neutral |
| ☐ Somewhat Agree | ☐ Somewhat Agree |
| ☐ Strongly Agree | ☐ Strongly Agree |

• Unrecognized need: "I don't have the need/desire to share."

| **Husband** | **Wife** |
|---|---|
| ☐ Strongly Disagree | ☐ Strongly Disagree |
| ☐ Somewhat Disagree | ☐ Somewhat Disagree |
| ☐ Neutral | ☐ Neutral |
| ☐ Somewhat Agree | ☐ Somewhat Agree |
| ☐ Strongly Agree | ☐ Strongly Agree |

# Four

**4**

# Facing Our Natural
Tendency to Avoid

# 19

# *Creating Change*

Charles, Trish, and I were meeting for our first session. Other than introductions and some benign conversation, very little had taken place. Then Charles ushered forth a pronouncement, "I wouldn't have initiated this." The *this* to which Charles was referring was counseling. I was aware that Trish had made the appointment for counseling. But I knew nothing about her, Charles, or the reason for the appointment. Charles's observation seemed to catch Trish a little by surprise. I was uncertain as to the reason for her surprise—had she just encountered new data from Charles or was she perplexed by his inappropriate choice of timing? His observation definitely did not fit the conversational context. However, I was more concerned about the meaning of Charles's comment.

Did Charles think that counseling was unnecessary for their situation? Did he dislike the idea of counseling in general? Was this an issue of privacy or pride? Or was he merely making a statement about his own behavioral tendencies, that he was basically passive by nature, tending to wait for others to initiate actions? There were several other different explanations that I could have hypothesized. The important point, however, was to realize that the reason could make a difference in the course of counseling.

Trish began to explain what had caused her to make the appointment. There had not been a crisis event; Charles had done nothing out of the ordinary. But Trish had finally faced the emerging awareness of a gnawing feeling of unrest. "It's a problem with things in general." Trish used the word *stuck* several times as she described what for her had been a long history of marital disappointments that had increasingly produced a feeling of general dissatisfaction. Gradually, their relationship had journeyed to their present static condition that Trish could only describe as stuck.

> I've been operating under the illusion that things will someday get better. It finally hit me that this may not be the case. I've been stuffing my dissatisfaction for years. That's probably made me depressed. I don't know. Maybe it has and maybe it hasn't. All I know is that I'm tired of living this way.
>
> Something has to change. Whether it's me, Charles, our marriage, or my illusion—things just can't go on as they have been. That's why I'm here. You'll have to ask Charles why he's here. All I know is I'm ready to make a responsible decision about my marriage. I think if Charles were to be honest, he'd say the same thing. We both need some relief.
>
> If my marriage is not going to get any better, I need to know that. I can deal with reality. I just need to know what it is. I would prefer that we take our relationship to the next level. But there seems to be a barrier between us. Something seems to be stopping our being able to do that on our own. So I thought it was time to see a professional.

Charles listened intently as Trish shared her concerns. She described a marriage with a great deal of distance, both emotional and relational. Trish wanted a closer relationship: "I need attention—connectedness—intimacy. I need it both emotionally and physically. Charles seems to find this difficult to do." When she had finished, I asked Charles to state his perspective. He agreed with much of Trish's description of their marriage as a static, unconnected union. Then he went on to state his fears.

> We don't talk. That's a fact. And I hear Trish's words when she talks about taking our relationship to the next level. But I don't know

that I really understand it. Neither do I know if we can get it there. That's what scares me. What happens if we can't? What does that mean for us?

Charles was intelligent. He had demonstrated this through both academic and career accomplishments. I realize, though, that people can be exceptionally competent in some areas but grossly lacking in others. So it was possible for Charles to be at once intellectually accomplished and emotionally illiterate. However, I doubted that to be the case in this situation. I suspected that Charles's lack of understanding was more a case of his playing dumb rather than being dumb. As Charles continued to speak, he began to clarify my suspicions.

Trish wants us to be closer. There are lots of external things in our life that automatically interfere with that—kids, jobs, no time, no money. But what really concerns me is whether I am capable of doing what's called for. Trish wants me to open up. As she puts it, she wants me to let her into my life. I hear what she says. I just don't understand what that is. How exactly do you let someone into your life?

I wasn't raised that way. Home was a battle zone—a place that I endured. I learned to protect myself—to not open up. I don't even know if that's the way I'm constructed. You know, that male stuff. I know that I don't share. But that's the way I am. I can't help it. What can you do if that's the way you are?

## More Justification

Charles made no attempt to deny his lack of self-disclosure. He also admitted his tendency to avoid dealing with dissatisfactions. His statement, "But that's the way I am," may have even been the truth. My problem is not so much with the accuracy of Charles's words as with the hidden implications in them. I suspected Charles possessed an attitude that would prove to be problematic, an attitude that, if allowed to persist, would make the potential for any real future change appear bleak.

Charles had an air of justification. He felt that his freely admitted avoidant behavior was both legitimate and somehow beyond the realm of his responsibility. After all, he reasoned, how could he help but be avoidant? Through parental and family modeling, the crucible of life's experiences, genetic and God-ordained predispositions, or whatever else might seem plausible as a rationale, he was the way he was supposed to be. He couldn't help it. Influences beyond his control had made him the way he was.

This attitude of justification had a domino effect on Charles's marriage. His belief that he was neither responsible for who he was nor for changing anything about himself limited what could be expected of the future. Trish had already voiced the realization that she had been living in an illusion. Though she could probably adapt to a relationship that was far less than she had previously hoped for, I doubted that continuing in a marriage that was emotionally stuck was quite the reality that she could accept. But if Charles failed to assume any responsibility for amending his behavior, the prognosis for any real change in the future appeared dismal.

Change was needed in this marriage, but it did not appear that it would come either quickly or easily. In reality, however, this difficulty for Charles and Trish is more the norm than the exception. Little was different in their marriage than would be found in most. If making personal and relational changes were all that easy to accomplish, there would be fewer books written about marriage and fewer couples seeing counselors.

Change does not easily occur because of two predictable obstacles, resistance and natural interference. The dilemma presented by Charles was a clear example of the more difficult of the two—*resisting* change. But, as we will observe, neither blockage is necessarily easy to resolve.

## What Really Stops Us?

A colleague of mine has stated that the real art of therapy is not in figuring out what people ought to do, it is in getting them to do it. This is what I have been suggesting throughout most of this chapter. Change is possible, but it is also difficult. What really stops us from doing what we need to do, even when we know that we ought to?

## Our Basic Nature

Part of our difficulty with change rests with our basic nature. We are creatures of habit and comfort. We like stability and predictability. The tranquil moorings of the harbor are preferred to the rough seas. In our personal lives, we achieve a constant level of predictability in our relationships. We get into a rhythm. Because of our desire for comfort, we naturally tend to maintain the present situation rather than venturing into uncharted seas. We do not like to rock the boat, and we resist any attempt to change what we have grown to embrace as the norm.

For change to occur in a relationship, something must rock the boat. Something has to place enough force on us to break us loose from the moorings that hold us so peacefully in the harbor. However, this disruption will not lead to a continual life of upheaval, although this may be a fear. The disruption will actually be short-lived. Couples tend to establish a new comfort level after any disruption. If the pressure to change was unsuccessful, the couple may do little more than return to the old way of doing things. If the pressure was successful, however, there may actually be a change to an improved level of interacting.

This disruptive pressure may come from either outside forces, inside forces, or a combination of the two. Charles and Trish illustrated a combination of both outside and inside forces at work in their relationship. Charles was experiencing outside pressure to change—Trish was making it quite clear that she was tired of their marriage as it was. She wanted to see the relationship changed, so she was rocking Charles's boat. The pressure at work on Trish was of an internal nature. The desire for change emerged from deep inside her. She had finally reached a point where the internal desire for something to be different had caused enough personal disruption to rock her own boat.

Charles and Trish also illustrated a basic marital principle. Couples change when their comfort level is challenged enough to allow them (individually and together) to successfully develop new ways of behaving. There are many factors that influence whether any attempt at change will be successful or not. One important factor is the form and amount of resistance to change that arises within the individuals and the relationship.

Will the couple adapt their behavior? Or will they cling to things as they are? This will be largely determined by their resistance to change, which emerges in two distinct forms, natural interferences and classical resistance.

## Natural Interferences

There is a pureness in natural interferences—no hidden agendas, no deceptions, nothing malignant. Nonetheless, they still interfere. They make it easier to do what you have always done than what is best. Natural interferences make doing what is healthy a chore; that requires intentional effort.

If this form of resistance to change were placed in an attitude statement, it would be something like this: "I want to change—but it is difficult." The want to is present. But something natural, making any change in behavior difficult, is also present.

A prime example of a natural interference is the relational homeostasis and equilibrium that was just discussed. Couples naturally establish a way of relating. There is a comfort that accompanies this predictability. Any attempts to change these established rules for interacting are a threat to the couple's tranquil normality. This change would require energy and involve risk. Who could predict what the relationship might look like if change were permitted? So change is naturally resisted.

Another form of natural resistance is more individual. Whether due to genetic predispositions, cultural influences, or personal experiences, a mate may find a particular behavior, regardless of how healthy it might be, to be personally uncomfortable. This personal discomfort acts as a natural interference. A client once told me, "Emotions make me uncomfortable." He was referring to either his sharing of emotions or being around someone else who was sharing. He simply found emotions frightening. This personal discomfort stood in the way of easily changing his behavior and acted as a block to his improving the level of intimacy in his marriage.

Natural interferences can be anticipated, and they can be difficult, but at least they are honest. It is their forthrightness that makes them easier to face and resolve than the next category. The characteristics of those interferences labeled as classical resistance are significantly more of a challenge.

## *Classical Resistance*

Unlike those who have a natural interference of some kind, there is no pureness in those who exhibit classical resistance to change. There is only malignancy. These spouses have an attitude. A statement that adequately represents this attitude would be: "I do not *really* want to change." The *want to* for change is not present. To the contrary, there is a definite intent to resist that goes far beyond the realm of mere personal discomfort. Sometimes the intent to resist is clearly stated. At other times, the attitude is present but is either denied or concealed, as in the case of Charles and Trish. Charles's intent to resist change, evidenced in his attitude of justification, was never clearly or overtly expressed. Instead, it was presented indirectly, but was there, nonetheless.

At that first meeting, Charles's position in the relationship was one of classical resistance. He made it clear that he had no intention of changing anything about his behavior. He was present at the meeting primarily to appease Trish. He wanted to appear cooperative and interested in the future development of his marriage, but what he really wanted was for Trish to settle down—to allow things in their relationship to return to the calm that had preceded this crisis. He had no desire to behave any differently. Nor did he have any desire for the relationship to be any different. But he did not want to state this directly, so he mentioned being confused about what Trish wanted and, based on a myriad of rationales, even questioned his potential for change. If Charles had been honest, he would have stated his real goal—that things just get back to the way they were.

Classical resistance stems from a variety of causes, none of them good. For example, some resistant spouses are simply selfish. They are takers, not givers. They like having things their own way and being taken care of; they dislike responsibility and put down the concept of mutuality. Unless there is a basic change in their personalities, these individuals do not make good spouses and are extremely difficult to live with.

Sometimes classically resistant spouses are harboring resentment. Their initial anger from previous relational injuries was never resolved. This failure resulted in a blockage in the marriage. In this instance, resentment, rather than a character flaw, is what fuels any resistance to change.

Other resistant spouses simply do not care enough for the other person in the relationship to put forth any effort. One client, who was later found to have been deceptively having an affair during the process of therapy, made the statement, "This is just too hard for me to do." What he really meant was, "I'm not interested enough in you to make the effort."

Sometimes classically resistant spouses have control difficulties, another example of a personality issue. These spouses do not like following instructions of any kind or being told what to do. Expectations are equated to demands and are to be resisted at all cost. So the idea that they might have to change something is totally rebuffed.

Classical resistance takes on many different forms. But all of them share in common a resilience to change—a resilience that extends beyond what is viewed as the more natural forms of interferences. However, like their more natural counterparts, they too are resolvable but require a greater effort.

## Looking Ahead

Creating change is difficult. But it is entirely possible. During the remainder of this section, we will explore some more specific ways to bring change to a relationship. Because all relationships are different and unique, not all of what will be presented will apply to your marriage. But there should be something for everyone.

While these remaining chapters will identify specifics, I will close this chapter with some generalities. If change is to come to your relationship, the following characteristics will be found somewhere in the process.

- You will have an understanding of what constitutes relational health. "What ought to be going on in our marriage?"

- You will be able to conduct an honest assessment of your own relationship and ask questions like, "What is good in our marriage and what needs to be improved?"
- Through working together, you will develop a plan of action to bring the desired change. "If we were serious about changing our marriage, what would we do?"
- You will identify what might interfere with your achieving change. "What are the natural interferences for us? Is there any resistance? What really stops us?"
- You will determine your level of commitment to taking control of your relationship. "Are we really committed to bringing change?"
- You will do what it takes to achieve your goal.

# 20

# *Taking Control of Avoidance*

Taking control of avoidance is a proactive statement. There is nothing passive about it because there is nothing passive about change. Change requires effort. If your intent is for things to improve with little effort on your part, you will be disappointed. Without effort and follow-through, the patterns and strategies that have operated in your relationship throughout most of your marriage will continue.

To state that a lack of effort will result in a corresponding lack of change is a little misleading. It would be more accurate to state that no constructive change will occur. Doing nothing will result in a change of sorts, just not the change that you desire. Passiveness will allow continued deterioration, because there is nothing to alter or prevent the natural erosion that comes as a result of avoidant lifestyles. The block to closeness will become more fortified, the pressure to push each other apart will become more intense, and the emotional distance that has created a void in your togetherness will grow increasingly larger.

Constructive change—the kind of influence that produces health—will cost you something. It may require that you give up comfort. It may require that you take a risk. Change is not a gift; it will require some effort. Some couples find that creating a plan of action specifically tailored to meet their needs helps direct their energy as they attempt to take control of their relationship.

These specifically tailored strategies are referred to as action plans. When fleshed out, the specifics that make up a particular couple's action plan will depend on their unique needs and their readiness for change. Some couples will require little outside help and influence. For example, they will find that simply the knowledge that avoidance tendencies are natural and that they interfere with the development of a healthy marriage will be enough of an influence for them to deal constructively with and change their relationship. It's as if this new insight gives them permission to make changes. Other couples, though enlightened with the same information, will require more assistance to take charge of their relationship. They will require more specific instruction such as a clear definition of what constitutes good communication and what constitutes bad. Some couples will find certain tasks helpful, others will not. In short, each may require different and varying influences in order to bring the needed changes. Some may even need the extra benefit derived from seeing a therapist in order to make the necessary changes. However, regardless of these differences in couples, the steps to change—the sequence required in taking control of their relationship—will remain the same.

## Steps to Taking Control

Change is a process that, as with most processes, involves many steps. The following summary is adapted from the structure I follow when treating avoidance in a therapeutic setting. Because you have a unique relationship, with a particular level of readiness, you will need to adapt—modify and/or intensify—the structure to meet your own personal requirements.

The steps required to bring about change are in three different but progressive stages. The first stage deals with *preparing* yourself for change. This is followed by the *commitment*—a formal resolution to do what is necessary to bring change to your relationship. The final stage is *work*—what you must actually do if change is to be achieved.

## Preparing for Change

In preparing for change, you are laying the foundation for the work to come. Real, lasting change requires a well developed foundation and is not usually the product of impulse or whim. It is deliberate. In preparing to actually work at changing your relationship, you must (1) define health, (2) assess your situation, and (3) face reality. Once these are completed, you are ready to proceed to the next stage in the change process.

### 1. Define health.

In *Alice in Wonderland* by Lewis Carroll, Alice and the Cheshire Cat have a conversation that resembles what far too often happens in our marriages.

> "Would you tell me, please, which way I ought to go from here?"
> "That depends a good deal on where you want to get to," said the Cat.
> "I don't much care where," said Alice.
> "Then it doesn't matter which way you go," said the Cat.

Uncertainty of destination can be a problem for marriages also. In order to deal with avoidance, couples need to understand where they are taking the relationship and why. The *where* of their ultimate destination is relational health. The *why* is because this destination will both enhance and safeguard their marriage. Understanding where and why, the question that remains for them to answer is, "*What* is health?"

I am constantly confronted with couples who do not understand marital health. More specifically, they are confused about what ought to be happening in a marriage if the relationship is to move in a healthy direction. Among other things, healthy relationships are characterized by good communication and growing intimacy. Spouses who practice good communication deal with each other in honest, direct, and appropriate manners. They are able to state their needs and talk about their dissatisfactions. And they are able to share what they feel and think. The result of good communication behavior is that couples increasingly find themselves growing closer together, and their marriages become more stable.

It is by understanding health that we are motivated to deal with avoidance. Avoidance interferes with the development of healthy and intimate relationships. It blocks communication through the creation of emotional barriers or walls, pushes spouses apart through the consequential development of resentment, and maintains emotional distance through the lack of self-disclosure. By defining health, we establish where we ought to be and why. This knowledge will prepare you to move to the next step in the process—examining your own situation. You are now ready to ask the question, "Where are we?"

### 2. Assess your situation.

In order to face and resolve any problem, it is important that you clearly identify what you are facing. When dealing with avoidance, two questions help bring the necessary clarity: "What am I doing?" and "Why am I doing it?"

The whats and the whys were identified earlier in this book when we contrasted behaviors with motivations. It is important to identify what you are doing. How are you being avoidant? Do you avoid dealing with conflict alone? With sharing alone? Or in both areas? It is also important to determine why you behave in this manner. This is accomplished by exploring and understanding the various motivations for the avoidance. What acts as an interference for you?

One means of assessing your situation is by utilizing the assessment exercises included in this book. An easy reference guide to these exercises is in the quick-quiz directory. These exercises offer you an opportunity to take an objective look at your relationship. For instance, the questions in the quick-quiz on page 70, Reflecting on Conflict Avoidance, will help you identify how you avoid dealing with conflict, whereas the quick-quiz on page 123, Identifying Your Motivation to Be Avoidant, focuses on why you choose to avoid conflict. Each Quick-quiz exercise, whether dealing with conflict avoidance or intimacy avoidance or the whats or the whys, is intended to provide you with quick and accurate information for answering the question, "What is going on in my relationship?"

In addition to these more objective assessment activities, you may choose to do something a little more subjective. Some couples prefer to assess their situation by taking their own marital pulse. To do this, they stop and take an introspective look at their relationship, paying particular attention to any red flags that may emerge during this self-evaluation. In particular, they ask a series of questions focusing on both emotional and behavioral themes.

Questions of an emotional nature might include:

- Am I feeling dissatisfied about anything in my marriage?
- Am I feeling lonely in my marriage?
- Does there seem to be an emotional distance between me and my spouse?
- Am I harboring any feelings of resentment?

Questions of a behavioral nature might include:

- Are there things happening in my marriage that are obviously inappropriate?
- Is there a lack of constructive activities in my marriage?
- Could I (or my spouse) be doing more to invest in our marriage?
- What am I doing about my feelings?

Regardless of the method you choose, whether objective, subjective, or a combination of the two, it is important that you honestly assess what is going on in your marriage. By working through the process of first understanding what *ought* to be happening in a healthy marriage, and then assessing what *is* happening in your own, you can move to the next step in the process—facing reality.

### 3. Face reality.

A colleague of mine has said, "Reality's what is." That may not be the most grammatically correct statement, but it is extremely profound. What she means by this statement can best be seen by recognizing what reality is not. Reality is not what we wish it to be. It is not fantasy, not a denial of the truth, and not what would be the best solution. When working on avoidance, the last step in preparing for change is to truly embrace reality. Clinging to wishes, fantasies, and denial won't let change happen. And to fail in this part is to fail in the whole.

In embracing reality, you are asking and answering the question, "How is it with us—really?" This involves a comparison of the facts. You already have all the information necessary to make this comparison by knowing what ought to happen and what is happening. Now, compare the two. The result is your reality.

The facts are the key to determining reality. You can wish that there was closeness in your marriage. You could fantasize and imagine that dissatisfactions are dealt with. And you can even have the best of intentions. But what are the facts? What is happening? It is with facts that we confront denial. In reality, what you say to be true and what is true are one and the same. If there is a difference, then you are living in denial. Facts help us to see the denial.

By facing reality and honestly owning what is happening in your relationship, you bring the preparation for change stage to a close. You are now ready to move to the next stage in the process of taking control of avoidance—commitment. Unlike the previous stage, what follows will require only one step. And it will focus more on making a decision than it will on self-assessment. But it is really the watershed of the change process. With commitment the corner is turned toward change.

### Making a Commitment

Commitment is one of those terms that people raised in the church grow up hearing. Familiarity does not always insure understanding, however. This is especially true when considering commitment in regard to marriage. In *The Drifting Marriage* (1988) and *Love Secured* (1994), I went to great lengths to describe what actually constitutes commitment in marriage. I pointed out the fact that in marriage there are actually two commitments. There is commitment to marriage as an institution—when spouses vow to remain together "til death do us part." There is also commitment to marriage as a relationship. That commitment is everything else that is pledged, "to honor, to cherish, to love. . . ." A true and complete commitment to marriage is one that is a dual commitment to marriage as an institution and a relationship, and not either one or the other.

The argument I presented in these books was largely theoretical. Being a pragmatist, I backed away from the theory and asked myself, "Exactly how do you measure these different commitments to marriage?" Answering this question about marriage as an institution was the easiest. You measure commitment to the institution by looking at divorce statistics. Are people staying married, regardless of what is going on in the relationship? I am reminded of a funny story in which Ruth Bell Graham was reportedly asked whether she would ever consider divorcing her husband, the famous evangelist Billy Graham. Her answer was a resounding no! "I believe too much in the sanctity of marriage to ever divorce Billy. I might shoot him. But I'd never divorce him." Mrs. Graham was describing commitment to an institution.

Determining how to measure commitment to marriage as a relationship is a more challenging task. After spending several months contemplating the question, I arrived at what I believe to be an accurate answer. You measure commitment to a relationship by the degree to which a spouse does what is in the best interest of the relationship as opposed to what is more comfortable personally. So if dealing with dissatisfaction is personally uncomfortable, what do you do? It depends on your level of commitment. If you are committed to your marriage as a relationship, you will deal with your spouse regarding your dissatisfaction despite your personal discomfort. If you are more committed to your level of comfort, you will avoid.

When preparing to take control of avoidance, there is a reason for facing reality. It is in facing reality that you are offered an opportunity to take responsibility for what you find. You are presented a choice. Are things going to continue as they have? Or are they going to be different? The decision is yours. And the ultimate choice generally boils down to one question—"Am I committed?"

The preparation stage was largely informational, looking at the facts. As we will soon see, the working stage is behavioral. It involves doing something. The commitment stage, under present consideration, is attitudinal. It involves making a choice—a resolution. Real commitments are not made while living in denial. They are made with a full knowledge of the facts—and often in spite of the facts. Also in spite of probable difficulties and personal discomfort, a resolution to pursue health and the best interest of the marriage becomes paramount. You decide that you will do what it takes— whatever that may be. Without such a commitment, it is not likely that you will go any further in this process. Are you committed to your marriage? Really committed? If your answer is yes, then you have turned a corner and you are ready to proceed. If not, it is not likely that change will come to your marriage.

## Creating Change

You have your information. You have determined what is right for a marriage, assessed what is actually occurring in your own relationship, and in comparing the two, discovered the discrepancies. Recognizing that change is needed, you have committed yourself to this end. It is now time to *do* something about it.

The final stage of taking control involves action. This is the working stage where change begins to physically take place. There are actually two steps involved in creating change. The first involves creating a plan of action. The second is simply to follow through with your plan.

### 1. Develop a plan.

There is an old saying that applies here—"If things aren't going according to plan, maybe there never was a plan." Though you may need little more than permission to totally and completely change your relationship, most of us will need a little more impetus and a plan of some kind. As a colleague has stated, you can have intimate experiences spontaneously. They are unexpected bonuses, and we enjoy them when they occur. But intimate relationships are the result of planning.

Working on change begins with developing a personal action plan. The operative term here is *personal*. And the rule of thumb is do what works for you. As an illustration, let me share something that happened to me when I decided to take up running. In my youth, I was both an avid and accomplished long-distance runner. A career-ending knee injury interrupted my plans to pursue the sport competitively in college. But several years later, when facing the choice of either growing old gracefully or going completely to pot, I decided to resume the activity.

It was amazing what had taken place in the field of running during those twenty years. What had once been a sport for only the foolhardy was now a national pastime. Everyone was a runner. And everyone with a pair of seventy-five-dollar running shoes and a multicolored warm-up suit was an expert. I started receiving all sorts of unsolicited advice: Run in the morning; run every day; run longer distances at a slower pace rather than shorter distances at a faster pace.

What did I end up doing? I did what worked best for me! I ran in the afternoon; it took until after lunch for my joints to even start working. Rather than running every day, I ran every other day. My chronic knee injury would not allow me to run any more frequently than that. And finding the longer and slower paced distances to be more boring, I opted to run the shorter but faster-paced distances. All of this was in direct contradiction to the advice I had been given, but it worked best for me.

When developing an action plan, you should bear the same attitude in mind. Do what works for you. Action plans are as varied and unique as the marriages for which they are created. Who knows your needs better than you? And who knows better than you what you are likely to do?

Though action plans are unique, they generally share some common themes. For example, action plans focus on making healthy choices. You choose to do what is best versus what is comfortable. In a similar vein, the healthy choices in these action plans force you to face your discomfort. Whether this discomfort is from dealing or sharing within the relationship, change will require that you confront the fear one way or another. However, this confrontation will not go unrewarded. Through experience, you learn that the dreaded consequence is not really a consequence after all. Finally, action plans are cooperative ventures. There is consensus among spouses. You work together as husband and wife to determine what you will and will not do. There are no ultimatums, no singularly determined strategies. Just each of you asking for and receiving help from the other.

A work sheet for creating your own action plan is provided at the end of this chapter on page 216. It includes some questions for you to answer and several blank lines. Action plans cannot be given to a couple; they must be created by the couple.

The final step in the change process, taking control, includes suggested activities for couples. Some of these may even find their way into your action plan, but the action plan will still be your own creation.

## 2. Take control.

Ultimately, all of your planning boils down to one question— "What are we going to do about avoidance?" The cry has been, "I love you—Talk to me!" What will be your response? Will things continue as they have, or will there be change? For change to occur, you will have to do something different from the past. This final step in the change process, taking control of avoidance, requires that you follow through on both your commitment and action plan.

It is difficult to make generic task assignments because marriages exist in such diverse situations. What I will do is make observations about some of the things that I do when working with couples in counseling. Obviously, these situations require outside intervention whereas yours may not. But some of these activities, at least in adapted form, will prove helpful for you as well. One particular activity may be used in a less intense manner, or you may be able to make some constructive changes without outside encouragement. This is where your creative powers will come into play.

### Dealing and Sharing

One of the things I do in counseling sessions is offer couples the opportunity to do the very things they have difficulty doing on their own. If their difficulty is facing conflict, I have them deal with a particular dissatisfaction in the counseling session. If their difficulty is with self-disclosure, I have them talk and share. They learn from this experience of having to face what is difficult.

Frequently, I assign homework for couples to do that involves dealing and sharing away from the therapy setting. Obviously, I have more control in the counseling session over whether they actually deal and share than I do when they are at home. If they try to quit too soon in my office, I can direct their attention back to the task at hand. At home they are on their own. However, I never give a homework assignment that I do not follow up on. The first thing I do at the next session is ask for a status report.

Scheduling opportunities to deal and share could be a vital part of your action plan. Exactly how you decide to do this is entirely up to you. Some couples set specific times during the week for the sole purpose of taking their relational pulse, asking each other, "Is there anything we need to deal with or share?" Then they take the time to honestly relate. Others prefer more spontaneity and less structure. Rather than holding things in reserve until an appointed time, they agree to deal or share whenever either of them draws attention to that need. Whether a spouse becomes aware of a personal dissatisfaction or senses the possibility of a dissatisfaction in the other, he or she immediately brings it to the spouse's attention. Because this is a previously agreed upon plan of action, the spouse automatically responds in an honest manner. The end result of activities like these is a change in behavior. Together, spouses commit to a plan that enables them to face their fears, and as a result, they take control of their avoidance.

## Learning New Skills

I try to teach clients new skills. Though spouses learn from their experiences, such as having to deal and share, a more direct form of instruction can also be helpful. Whether this instruction emphasizes how to effectively communicate, deal assertively, or any number of other skills, they can be learned and practiced in a therapist's office.

The idea of learning new skills has great application to action plans. The resources available for learning are innumerable. For instance, the needs of a couple could easily be met by reading a book or listening to a tape. Other couples may also benefit from reading a book but may require something a little more intensive. They may find training groups and topical seminars more helpful.

### EXPLORING ORIGINS

I routinely explore the origin of a spouse's natural interference. The motivation for being avoidant can usually be traced to something historical. For instance, it is frequently linked to relationship patterns learned in a spouse's family or other childhood experiences outside the home. A little history provides a great deal of information about experiential themes and behavioral patterns. We learn a lot as children. And just because we enter adulthood does not mean that we leave all we learned in the past. We tend to carry the past with us and repeat what we have learned in our new relationships.

Exploring the origins of avoidance is an effective means of bringing change. There is nothing magical about identifying origins. And the tendencies do not simply disappear once they are brought to light. Nor should there be any attempt to absolve an individual of any personal responsibility for being avoidant by identifying the reason for his or her behavior. We do not profit from simply finding someone or something to blame. We discover the reasons in order to begin change.

Insight alone does not bring change. But understanding the reasons for avoidance can give a spouse the opportunity to take responsibility for what he or she discovers. An appropriate utilization of reasons is the following statement, "Regardless of why or how I got this way, only I can change it." Following this same theme, I sometimes ask clients the question, "How long are you going to let this control your life?" This is not an attempt to be cruel, only to reinforce the theme of personal responsibility.

Recognizing the origins of your avoidance tendencies can be extremely helpful, and this is not something that necessarily requires a therapist to accomplish. Husbands and wives can be quite adept at working together to discover their own reasons. Once again, other resources may prove helpful. Some retreats will focus on these kinds of issues, as will some seminars. Books, too, can be helpful. But regardless of the particular aid utilized, this area is fertile ground for joint discussion.

### CHALLENGING INTERFERENCES

Challenging a particular motivation or interference always involves offering information that more accurately represents the truth. It is hoped that this new information will result in a changed perspective and thus changed behavior.

Challenging interferences is a two-step process. The first must be a clear identification of the particular interference, and the second must present information that directly challenges this perception. For example, if a client's tendency to avoid conflict is maintained by the belief that avoidance is the proper thing to do, it is imperative that I determine the specific misbelief that supports this position. Is it a spiritual issue?—"It is unchristian to hurt people's feelings." Is it a lack of understanding regarding what constitutes healthy relationships?—"It is best to not have a fuss for any reason. Arguments only lead to strained relationships." The possibilities for misbelief are enormous. But in order to provide the appropriate correcting information, the specific misbelief must be identified.

How will challenging interferences work for you? That will depend entirely on how well entrenched the particular interference is. Sometimes recognizing the truth is a simple process. Through reading a book or hearing a tape, you are presented with a new insight. You might even say to yourself, "Wow! I never saw it that way before. That makes perfect sense." You then incorporate the new information and begin changing your life. The change may be small at the beginning, but little beginnings can have significant effects on a relationship.

Sometimes motivations are more firmly entrenched. Maybe they have been a part of your life for many years. These will require a more concerted—and possibly repetitive—effort. Entrenched motivations may require that you personally challenge them on a regular basis because the "aha" experience of reading a book just didn't take on the first exposure. It's not that you do not have the new insight, it's just hard getting rid of the old. Or maybe you will choose to discuss the problem with your spouse each time it appears. Do what works. Just remember the two steps—identify and then challenge.

CHALLENGING RESISTANCE

Challenging interferences and challenging resistance require totally different interventions. The key to understanding the difference between these two is contrasting their origins. Both block the development of intimacy in a marriage, but an interference is natural in origin and resistance is a mutation. The real differentiating factor is attitude. A spouse whose movement toward closeness is blocked by a natural interference would be represented by the following attitude: "I want to change—but it is difficult."

The desire to do what is best is evident, but it is difficult. This is not the case with classical resistance. A spouse who is resistant would be represented by the following attitude: "I do not really want to change."

With this spouse, the desire for change is absent. This could be for several different reasons, from personality difficulties to resentment. Depending on the particular spouse, resistance may be stated directly, thus leaving little doubt that it is occurring, or it may be played out more indirectly. When resistance is indirect, it prompts confusion in the spouse.

Indirect resistance can be displayed in several ways. For example, a resistant spouse may drag his feet, act confused, or have an unusually difficult time completing what would appear to be simple tasks. As a rule of thumb, when identification and correction of natural interferences have brought no change in the relationship, I always explore the possibility of resistance. I do this by making a statement and asking a question, "Changing your relationship shouldn't be this difficult. What's really stopping you from making headway in your marriage?"

These are questions that can be incorporated in your own plan of action. When things are not progressing, there is a reason. Maybe something else has been overlooked, but it may also be resistance. Ask yourself and your spouse, "What is really going on here?" How you proceed will depend on the content and honesty of your answer.

## Summary

"I love you—Talk to me!" These are optimistic words. They express hope, love, and desire. And they define what needs to happen if a relationship is to grow. Are you ready to build a relationship instead

214 Facing Our Natural Tendency to Avoid

of blocking it? Are you ready to become more intimate—to draw closer? Then you have to be ready to deal with avoidance.

Taking control of avoidance is a process that requires only three things—knowing where you want to go, committing yourself to the journey, and making the trip. Two work sheets have been included at the end of this chapter to aid you in your process. The first is the Readiness Checklist. It will help you determine whether you are ready to develop an action plan. The second work sheet, Our Action Plan, will help you determine exactly what the process will require from you.

There is nothing magical about either of these work sheets. Neither is there anything sacred. Do not be limited by them. But if change is needed in your marriage, it is important that you do something.

## *Readiness Checklist*

Together, read and answer each question. It is important that you discuss each thoroughly. This is no time for pat responses. Honestly state what you believe and feel.

YES   NO   1. Do we understand what health is, and are we in agreement on what ought to be happening in a healthy marriage?

YES   NO   2. Do we recognize who is doing what when it comes to avoidant behavior—what is happening in our marriage?

YES   NO   3. Do we understand why we do what we do—what our motivations for being avoidant are?

YES   NO   4. Are we accepting reality and not clinging to denial?

YES   NO   5. Are we firmly committed to doing what is best for our marriage?

YES   NO   6. Are we willing to put time and effort into changing things in our marriage?

YES   NO   7. Are we ready to develop an action plan aimed at taking control of our avoidant tendencies, one that we both agree to?

YES   NO   8. Are we ready to follow through on implementing our action plan?

If you jointly answered YES to each of these questions, you are ready to develop an action plan for your marriage. If you failed to answer YES on an item, or there was not consensus, it is important to resolve the issue. You can still work on your marriage if consensus has not been reached; however, developing an action plan is not likely.

# Our Action Plan

Action plans are a cooperative effort. Together, answer each of the following questions and develop your own personal plan that will work for you.

*Identified tendencies:*

| Husband | is conflict avoidant. | Yes | No |
| | is intimacy avoidant. | Yes | No |
| | | | |
| Wife | is conflict avoidant. | Yes | No |
| | is intimacy avoidant. | Yes | No |

*Identified motivations for being conflict avoidant:*

Husband_____ Wife_____

*Identified motivations for being intimacy avoidant (interferences to sharing):*

Husband_____ Wife_____

*Challenges of the identified motivations and interferences:*

Husband_____ Wife_____

*Plan for creating change:*

How are you going to change the avoidance strategies?_____

_____

What will each of you do?_____

_____

What will each of you need from the other?_____

_____

What special aid(s) will you utilize? (books, seminars, training opportunities, structured time together, etc.)

_____

_____

_____

# 21

## Change

### Simple, but Not Easy

Recognizing what is required for a marriage to make a creative leap toward health is often easy. But doing it—making the creative leap—frequently becomes the difficult part.

Dawn, Kris, and I had already met for a few sessions. For the most part, these meetings had been devoid of any real emotional intensity. There had been a few tears, but that was all. This lack of intensity had not been because of any instruction on my part. It appeared to be more the manner in which Dawn and Kris were accustomed to relating. The sessions had focused on establishing a therapeutic relationship and gathering some important information including their respective complaints about the marriage, what had gotten them to this point, and what each of them wanted from counseling. But the tone had been cordial; even the complaints that each had were presented more as concerns for the relationship than attacks on each other. Both seemed to be in exceptional control of their emotions. At least this had been the case until the end of our last session. It was then that Dawn displayed some of her truer feelings, and in response, Kris too had taken a step toward greater honesty.

What had finally emerged in our last session was Dawn's "laundry list" of marital disappointments. Some of these dated as far back as the beginning of their marriage. Over time, she had allowed these disappointments to fester. Dawn now had a significant amount of resentment toward her husband. Kris bristled when Dawn became emotional in the session. He had been aware that Dawn had harbored some things from their past—events and acts that she seemed to have particular difficulty letting go. But he was not aware of all of her complaints. Neither was he entirely sympathetic. "I'm tired of Dawn's resentments coming in the way of our relationship," he said, then asked Dawn, "When are you going to let these go?"

There had been an obvious tension in the marriage, and Kris and Dawn were finally allowing this reality to surface. We spent some time talking about resentment and how it interferes with the growth of a marriage. We also discussed reconciliation and how it brings healing within a relationship. I then allowed Kris's statement regarding Dawn's resentment to set the agenda for our next session. With reconciliation as our goal, Dawn was asked to bring in her laundry list of resentments. My plan was for them to face, and hopefully resolve, everything that Dawn had been harboring. All in all, this type of agenda did not have the makings of a particularly enjoyable session.

Because of a holiday season, it had been several weeks since our last meeting, and there was some catching up to do. An atmosphere of calm pervaded the session as Dawn and Kris informed me of the events of the past weeks. The exchanges between them were pleasant, but I sensed that both Dawn and Kris were hesitant to proceed to the day's agenda. This is usually the case when the interval between sessions has been pleasant. The prevailing attitude becomes, "Why rock the boat?" But there was a need to deal with and resolve the issues. The calm was only an illusion. Without genuine resolution of the block between Kris and Dawn, it would be only a matter of time before something else would precipitate a crisis in their marriage.

I needed to set the stage for what was going to occur during the session, so I prefaced the interchange. First, I provided a rationale for why we were doing what we were doing. I reminded Kris and Dawn of what had brought them to counseling, what needs to happen in a relationship for it to grow and become more intimate, what seemed to be blocking growth in their marriage, and what I had asked them to do in order for us to resolve this block. Moving closer to the day's agenda, we then discussed the difference between for-

giveness and reconciliation. There needed to be a clear understanding of both roles—the forgiver and the forgivee.

Kris and Dawn were conversant with me during this portion of
the session. Each acknowledged understanding. With the staging
accomplished, it was time to begin the work. I asked Dawn to begin
sharing from her list. That was when things grew silent. Dawn froze.
The hesitancy I suspected now became obvious. Sensing she would
eventually say something, I allowed the silence to continue. Finally,
she began to speak to Kris.

> I'm afraid of what you might do. I don't want you to leave me, Kris,
> but I'm afraid that what I have to say might hurt you. And I'm also
> afraid of rocking the boat. It's been so good lately.
>
> (A pause. Then she addressed me.) This is so hard! It's not what
> I was raised to do. I was raised to just pretend that it doesn't bother
> me and then just let it go. But that's what has gotten me to this
> point so far.
>
> I know what I've been doing. And I know what I need to do. But
> still, it's just so hard to do!

I understood Dawn's dilemma. It was common. She was experiencing face to face the difference between something being simple
and being easy. The solution to Dawn and Kris's situation was simple enough. There needed to be healing in the relationship between
them. This would come through genuine reconciliation. Achieving
reconciliation would require actions and responsibilities on Kris's
part. He would have to own what was his responsibility, offer demonstrated remorse, and ask for Dawn's forgiveness. But Dawn would
also have to behave responsibly. She would have to face Kris with
her hurt. She needed to be heard and to know that she counted, but
it was with her part of this process—facing Kris—that she struggled.

## The Dilemma of Change

For Kris and Dawn, the solution for bringing some resolution to
the block in their relationship was simple, it just wasn't easy. The
same could be said for the general tendency to be avoidant that was

so evident in the relationship. As Dawn alluded, avoidance was something she was taught to do. "I was raised to just pretend it doesn't bother me." Whether Dawn was to deal with either her present level of resentment toward Kris or her long-term and historical pattern of avoidance, she was faced with the same dilemma. She could either continue in her past behavior and choose to not change, or she could do something different, thus making a choice for change. However, for change to occur, it would probably be necessary that she do something she would prefer not to do. Having to do something that we would prefer not to do is always the dilemma presented by the prospect for change.

Two truths emerge whenever the dilemma for change is presented. The first truth involves boundaries. No one can take your responsibility. This was illustrated by Dawn. There was no way for the resentment that she felt toward Kris to be resolved without her doing something about it. Kris could not do it for her. He had his own set of responsibilities to fulfill. This issue of boundaries was also true for changing the avoidance tendencies in her marriage. No one could take on her responsibility in this either.

The second truth involves cost. Change will always cost you something. Change will require something from you, if nothing more than personal discomfort. At least it will initially. It is hoped that the payoff from change is ultimate improvement. But that may be a long time in coming. Dawn found change very uncomfortable initially. This was due in part to her family rules. Dealing with Kris was contradictory to the way she had been raised. But another part of Dawn's discomfort came from the fear she had regarding what confrontation might end up doing to her marriage. Though her fear was excessive—the possibility existed even if the probability did not—the fear was still present. It required quite an effort on her part to do the best thing in spite of feelings to do otherwise.

Having feelings of discomfort like those Dawn had is not unusual. Though specific feelings may vary, if you are facing change, you will be faced with the dilemma of ultimately having to do something you would prefer to avoid. But the truths that no one else can take your responsibility and that change will always cost you something are balanced with the fact that it is only through facing problems that they can be resolved. The key to mastering the dilemma of change is found in looking beyond the immediate to the end result. It is the long-term benefit that we strive for.

## Kris and Dawn

"I know what I've been doing. And I know what I need to do. But still, it's just so hard to do!" This was Dawn's dilemma. So what did she decide to do? After a few moments of hesitation, Dawn decided to face her personal discomfort and her fears, and began talking to Kris about the hurts that she had been harboring for much of their marriage. This allowed for reconciliation, and the process of true healing within their relationship was begun.

The reconciliation process was not without its moments. Neither Dawn nor Kris was especially good at playing the necessary roles. Nor was the session without tension. In fact, it was quite intense. Dawn began to cry at the outset. She shared events and how they had hurt her. Kris listened but provided little response at first. As a part of our preparation for the session, I had cautioned him not to immediately find a defense for his actions. "We don't need 'Yes, but . . .' responses," I had told him. "We need for you to own what is your responsibility. And when you own something, Dawn needs to know that you're sorry. This is what reconciliation is all about."

Possibly for the first time in their marriage, Kris was really listening to Dawn. He was hearing her concerns. And it was apparent that what he was hearing was having an effect on him. He did not seem to know how to deal with what he was hearing, but they were definitely connecting.

I began to help Kris express what he was feeling. It wasn't long before Kris no longer needed my assistance. Dawn would cry, she would share, and she would get upset. Kris would listen, then respond that he did not know or he did not intend, and he was sorry. Forgiveness would be extended and then they would move on.

Kris and Dawn got better at dealing with the resentments and the process of reconciliation as the session progressed. Finally, they were through. Dawn had constructed a combination time line and treasure map with her list of hurts. The treasure, which would be attained if each hurt was resolved, was peace in their marriage. Both felt they had found the treasure by the end of the session. And both were also emotionally spent. Reconciliation can be an exhausting experience. They had enough energy to end the session with a hug—probably the most sincere touching they had expressed in several years.

Reconciliation is a beautiful thing. But as the situation with Kris and Dawn illustrates, it can be quite uncomfortable. At least beginning and continuing the process can be taxing, but the end result is well worth the effort.

## Final Thoughts

Nothing in this book has been particularly difficult to understand. Health is this. Being unhealthy is that. If you're doing what is healthy, continue. If you're not, change your behavior. The solution to the problem of avoiding conflict is for spouses to begin dealing with each other. The solution to the problem of avoiding intimacy is for spouses to become more self-disclosing. This is all very simple. It's just not always easy.

Things in general are seldom as simple as they seem, and life in particular is always more complex than it appears. If conflict avoidance is a natural tendency, there is a reason—a why associated with the what. The same can be said of intimacy avoidance. The motivations and interferences for our avoidance may vary, but the consequence remains the same. When avoidance prevails, the intimacy in our relationships for which we earnestly long is blocked and our marriages are in jeopardy.

Seldom do we simply and automatically do what is in the best interest of our relationships. Though some will have less difficulty with this than others, we all must make the choice for health. In making this decision, two things must be recognized. We are ultimately the only ones who can take responsibility for our behavior, and the decision to change will cost us something, at least in the short term.

God is not arbitrary. He never gives us directives—dos and don'ts—that are not totally in our best interest. This is true for our lives as individuals and also for marriage. In marriage, the Lord's design involves honesty—not dishonesty. And it involves closeness—not distance. Avoidance prevents both of these from occurring—it interferes, it blocks. Whereas the consequence of avoidance is pain, the benefit of dealing and sharing is that we enter in to the Lord's design for marriage. God's design is His prescription for pain. It is preventative. As we pursue His design, we pursue God's best—and also what is best for us. With that as our goal, we move toward an intimate and fulfilling marriage. Without it, we settle for far less.

# Notes

Chapter 2: The Problem of Avoidance

1. I have borrowed the terms "conflict avoidance" and "intimacy avoidance" from Emily Brown, a therapist in Washington, D.C.

Chapter 4: I Believe . . .

2. Donald Joy, *Bonding: Relationships in the Image of God* (Waco: Word Books, 1985), ix.

Chapter 17: Role Misperception: Interference #4

3. Dr. John Gray, *Men Are from Mars—Women Are from Venus* (San Francisco: HarperCollins, 1992).